英语科研论文写作

姜全红 孙 梅 王 萌 主编

Academic Writing
for Scientific Research in English

清华大学出版社
北京

内 容 简 介

本书共 9 章，详细介绍学术写作之准备过程、写作步骤及后续工作，帮助学生熟悉学术写作流程；重点介绍学术论文的文体风格，学术论文各部分内容的写作要点和行文规范，同时还提供丰富的例句表达，供学生参考使用，以便提高他们的学术英语写作能力，实现其国际学术论文的发表。本教材有配套课件，读者可登录 www.tsinghuaelt.com 下载使用。

本书可以作为我国高校理工科专业本科生和研究生学术英语教学的课程教材，也可以作为科研人员和教师工作中的参考指南。

版权所有，侵权必究。举报：010–62782989，beiqinquan@tup.tsinghua.edu.cn。

图书在版编目（CIP）数据

英语科研论文写作 /姜全红，孙梅，王萌主编 . —北京 ：清华大学出版社，2023.11
ISBN 978–7–302–63910–7

Ⅰ. ①英…　Ⅱ. ①姜…　②孙…　③王…　Ⅲ.①科学技术—英语—论文—写作　Ⅳ. ① G301

中国国家版本馆 CIP 数据核字（2023）第 114671 号

责任编辑：刘 艳
封面设计：平 原
责任校对：王凤芝
责任印制：宋 林

出版发行：清华大学出版社
网　　　址：https://www.tup.com.cn, https://www.wqxuetang.com
地　　　址：北京清华大学学研大厦 A 座　　　　邮　　编：100084
社 总 机：010-83470000　　　　邮　　购：010-62786544
投稿与读者服务：010-62776969, c-service@tup.tsinghua.edu.cn
质量反馈：010-62772015, zhiliang@tup.tsinghua.edu.cn
印 装 者：天津鑫丰华印务有限公司
经　　销：全国新华书店
开　　本：185mm × 260mm　　　印　　张：12.25　　　字　　数：284 千字
版　　次：2023 年 11 月第 1 版　　　印　　次：2023 年 11 月第 1 次印刷
定　　价：54.00 元

产品编号：093401-01

前　言

2022年4月，习近平总书记在视察中国人民大学时指出，我国要建设具有中国特色的世界一流大学。大学是人才培养的摇篮，是科技创新的源头，因此，建设世界一流大学的本质就是培养具有科技创新能力的世界一流人才。科技创新能力是一个涉及科技创新全过程的综合能力体系，而其起始端就是科学研究能力，也称学术研究能力。欧美和日本等发达国家的大学都高度重视对学生学术研究能力的培养，我国进入"双一流"建设的大学也都把培养学生的科学研究能力作为核心任务。

由于英语是当今世界科学技术领域的通用语言，运用英语进行专业学习、科学研究和学术交流，是世界一流人才不可或缺的能力。相应地，培养学生运用英语开展科学研究和进行学术交流的能力，也就成为大学人才培养的基础目标，是大学本科和研究生学术英语教育的重要内容。

《英语科研论文写作》作为大学开展学术英语教学的课程支撑教材，系统介绍了科研学术写作的类型、过程、方法、要求、科研语言、策略、文献来源、引用注释、成果发表、科研伦理等。全书共9章，具体内容如下：

第1章：介绍了学术英语的概念、用英语进行科研学术写作的原因，以及国际和国内运用英语进行科研学术写作的发展状况等，目的是让学生对英语科研论文写作有一个整体的理解和把握，激发他们内在的学习动机。

第2章：介绍了科研学术写作的类型，重点介绍了几种主要的写作类型及其特点和要求，包括原创性研究论文、文献综述性论文、研究计划、学术会议论文摘要、学位论文、技术报告等。这些写作类型是学生在接受高等教育期间常用或必须掌握的。

第3章：介绍了科研学术写作的过程，包括如何选题、如何检索文献、如何构建论文框架，以及如何进行论文整体的撰写、修改、校对等。了解科研学术写作的过程能够帮助学生进行合理的时间规划和安排，避免因拖沓（科研学术写作过程中的常见现象）或者缺失环节而对写作质量产生影响。

第4章：以科研学术论文（其他类型相似）为例介绍了论文各个组成部分的撰写方法、写作要求、注意事项等。科研学术论文一般由引言、文献综述（或理论框架）、研究方法（数据、材料、结果等）、分析讨论及其他部分组成。每个部分的内容都承载着各自的功能，缺一不可，所有部分按照相应的逻辑顺序共同支撑形成一篇完整的科研学术论文。

第5章：介绍了科研学术写作中的语言特点（词汇、语态、句子结构、段落结构等）以及撰写中的一些写作策略和技巧。英语科研论文写作是由英语语言和专业内容两个方面共同构成的，不同的学科领域在科研学术写作中采用的语言特点和策略技巧会有异同。对比这些异同之处可以帮助学生了解和掌握自己学科领域的写作语言特点和策略技巧。

第6章：介绍了科研学术写作中的文献资料来源以及检索方法和策略。文献资料是科研学术写作最重要的基础，文献资料检索是最重要的基础性工作。一般认为，在科研学术写作的全部工作中，文献资料检索占了三分之一左右甚至更多的工作量。因此，进行科研学术写作必须了解文献资料的来源渠道以及相关文献的检索方法和策略。此外，灰色文献也是重要的文献资料来源，由于灰色文献不在学术文献数据库中收录，掌握和运用灰色文献的检索方法也是科研学术写作需要具备的能力要求。

第7章：介绍了科研学术写作中参考文献的引用方式、注释原则和注释方法。在国际学术界有多种参考文献注释体系，任何科研学术写作都必须遵循一种参考文献注释体系对所参考使用的文献进行适当的引用标注，这是国际惯例。本书介绍了目前最常见的几种注释体系：Harvard、Oxford 和 Vancouver。

第8章：介绍了科研学术论文在国际上发表的途径和国际投稿过程。科研学术写作的最主要目的是进行科研学术成果的交流，这也是人类知识创造和知识传播的过程。科研学术写作完成后，作者选择适当的途径和平台在国际上发表，能够促进科研成果的广泛交流，提高作者的国际学术影响力，进而帮助作者获得更多的科研学术资源。目前，国际学术期刊和国际学术研讨会是科研学术成果在国际上发表的两种主要途径和方式。

第9章：介绍了科研学术写作中的科研伦理和科研不端问题。科研不端行为作为科研活动中的一种不良现象，很早就受到了广泛关注，国际学术界以及世界各国都有严格的监管体系和惩罚措施。了解科研学术写作中的科研不端行为能够帮助学生避免在科研学术写作中出现科研不端行为而对自身造成不利影响。

本书在编写过程中参阅了大量来自国际学术数据库和互联网的文献资料，以确保教材内容知识的新颖性和时效性。同时，所有这些文献资料都对本书的编写提供了重要的启发和借鉴，笔者在最后的参考文献列表中进行了详细著录，以此表示对所有文献作者及其研究成果的尊重和感谢。本书可以作为我国高校理工科专业本科生和研究生学术英语教学的课程教材，也可以作为科研人员和教师工作中的参考指南。

主编
2023 年 5 月于北京

Contents

Chapter 5
Language Usage in Scientific Writing ················· 87

Chapter 6
Databases, Grey Literature and Searching Strategies ················· 105

Chapter 1

Introduction

Learning Objectives

After reading this chapter, you should be able to:

1. Distinguish academic English, academic writing, and scientific writing;
2. Understand the dilemmatic situation of academic writing;
3. Understand the role of English in scientific communication in the world.

Chapter Lead-in: At the starting point, this first chapter introduces some key terms crucial to the readers' overall understanding of the task of academic writing for scientific research in English. Academic English is the genre of English used in the world of research, study, teaching and universities. Academic writing is among the fundamental requirements for undergraduate and graduate students in their tertiary education as well as in their future career in scientific research. English is generally considered to be the lingua franca of the scientific community, therefore, the international understanding of scientific writing mainly refers to the scientific writing in English.

1.1 What Is Academic English?

1.1.1 Academic

The definition of "academic", according to the *Cambridge Dictionary*, is "relating to schools, colleges, and universities, or connected with studying and thinking, not with practical skills", "based on ideas and theories and not related to practical effects in real life".[1] There are more entries for the definition of "academic" in the *Merriam-Webster Dictionary* as: "of, relating to, or associated with an academy or school especially of higher learning", "of or relating to performance in courses of study", "very learned but inexperienced in practical matters", "based on formal study especially at an institution of higher learning", "of or relating to literary or artistic rather than technical or professional studies".[2]

1.1.2 Academic Language

Academic language refers to the oral, written, auditory and visual language conversancy necessary for effective learning in institutions of higher education and academic programs, i.e., it's the linguistic tool for seminars, lectures, journals and books. University students are expected to acquire and gain fluency in this language. Academic language, in contrast with "conversational" or "social" language, consists of various formal language skills, including vocabulary, grammar, punctuation, syntax, discipline-specific terminology, or rhetorical conventions, which give students access to knowledge and academic competence. Intelligent

---

1   Cambridge Dictionary. Academic. Retrieved January 23, 2021, from Cambridge Dictionary website.
2   Merriam-Webster Dictionary. Academic. Retrieved January 23, 2021, from Merriam-Webster Dictionary website.

and capable as students might be, they may also have difficulty at school if they fail to have a good command of some terms and concepts or learn how to convey their ideas in required ways.

1.1.3 Academic English

Academic English is the genre of English for the field of research, study, teaching and universities. It is designed to train students from institutions of higher learning to use language properly for study.

Academic English is relatively complex and renders ideas in an objective and precise way. It is commonly recognized to consist of the vital skills of literary analysis, the observance of reference systems, the ability of critical assessment, etc. Very often are the important academic vocabulary, phrases and complex grammatical structures employed in academic conversation and text. Academic English, to be specific, is composed of words and practices, often used in formal speech and circumstances.

Academic English is considered to be one of the most common forms of English for specific purposes. It is being employed if you read an academic journal or listen to a talk or a presentation about an academic subject in an academic setting. Even native English speakers have to acquire academic English as it is different from the English that is used on a daily basis.

To effectively use academic English, one must employ the most proper style for specific purposes and targeted audiences. It usually has the following features:

- It employs formal academic language and avoids colloquialisms;
- It often avoids "I" and is written in the third person and usually employs impersonal structures;
- It is objective and impartial, which means that everything you say must be proven and you will not have fixed ideas until you begin your research;
- It frequently employs the passive voice;
- It is cautious and tentative;
- Other writers may get lots of references in it;
- The texts are well organized;
- Paragraphs are well developed usually with a powerful topic sentence ahead;
- Linking words are used to make the text cohesive.

1.2 What Is Academic Writing?

Writing is primarily designed to communicate with others using selected language, to influence thoughts or stimulate action in specific ways. In comparison with other communicative channels, writing is more permanent and may exert more impact. Through evidence and argument, a piece of writing can convince the readers of its analysis and conclusions. In most universities, the progress and learning of students are also assessed via their written work.

1.2.1 Academic Writing

Academic writing is a formal style of writing, involving the writing of articles, books, chapters, conference presentations, monographs, reviews, etc., and is used in universities and scholarly publications by professors, researchers and students from all disciplines to convey ideas, make arguments, and engage in scholarly conversation. A set of activities and methods are employed in academic writing, such as constructing, deconstructing and reconstructing knowledge, connecting, disconnecting and reconnecting concepts, describing and re-describing our views of the world, as well as shaping, misshaping and reshaping ideas. Academic writing may overlap with academic research and can make significant contribution to knowledge making.

Academic writing features evidence-based arguments, accurate word choice, logical organization and an impersonal tone. For most university students, getting a good command of academic writing is a challenging task, because they must conquer various hardships; to start with, they have not developed a consciousness of cognitive and meta-cognitive strategies for the academic writing process, and neither have they got familiar with academic genres or scholarly language characteristics.

1.2.2 Dilemmatic Situation of Academic Writing

Different disciplines require different genres of academic writing, so neither experts in academic writing nor specialists in a discipline can independently help students fully develop writing ability in their academic disciplines. However, hardly have discipline specialists and writing specialists had constructive collaboration. And scarcely are the two functions of generic academic writing and disciplinary writing combined through being taught by an expert in the discipline with additional specialized knowledge in academic writing. To make it worse, neither are the rules expressed explicitly. Therefore, it is a daunting task to guide students into successful academic writing in their disciplines.

Admittedly, some students still lack generic writing skills and may need to attend general writing courses; however, it may be high time that they move on to the complex writing practices at the university degree level, form collaboration among disciplinary experts, writing specialists and themselves, and clarify their proper roles in improving the skills of students in academic writing within a discipline.

In addition, as words are the basic building blocks of writing, understanding of words may also pose a problem to academic writing, including their translation into different languages. Scholarly writing often involves references to and translations from articles in other languages, and translation unavoidably increases the uncertainties, especially for those competent in only one language. Not only may words, common in one language, have no equivalents in others, but thinking processes also vary in different languages. In academic writing, when students encounter the use of translation from unfamiliar languages, there are no easy solutions to this problem.

1.3 What Is Scientific Writing?

1.3.1 Scientific Writing

One of the vital aspects of science lies in the sharing and exchanging results of scientific experiments. Either via open letters in early times or via telephone or email in the modern time, scientists, as long as they have completed the experiments and finished the analysis, need to formally share the new information with a bigger audience, so that other researchers may put this information to use, in which way their own experiments and research can be conducted.

To have a journal article published is one of the most common means for scientists to make their research formally known. The journal article acts as a component of the formal written document of the scientific process. Journals have remained the primary way of communication in the sciences, ever since 1665 when the first scientific journals made their appearance. Therefore, writing is a vital part of a researcher's career. Writing helps file and exchange ideas, activities and results to others and moreover is conducive to advancing science.

At present, the majority of scientific journals prefer to publish peer-reviewed articles. Through peer review, the reliability of published journal articles can be guaranteed. When an article is submitted to a journal, 2 or 3 people (called referees or reviewers) with expertise of the research topic are asked by the journal to review the article. Through scrutinizing the article, they make sure that the experiment is designed well and done accordingly; they go over the analysis of the data; they ascertain whether the data can justify the conclusion and they verify whether other scientists can understand the article. They also have a say in how much importance the article is of. It is the reviewers who guarantee that a good science article gets to meet a wide readership while the not-so-good one finds no way into the science journals.

Scientific research gets communicated to different audiences through scientific writing. Typically description and analysis are included in scientific writings, including surveys of former research and descriptions of present methodologies and results; and analysis connected with the trends, importance and implications of research findings. Though facts and meticulous reasoning are important in scientific writing, skills of successful communication must be used to polish their presentation in an appealing and convincing way. A good command of scientific writing may not come easily and only with practice can mastery be attained.

1.3.2　Scientific Writing in English in the World

At present over 90% of all scientific articles published are done in English and so are nearly all activities in science and technology. Therefore, English is universally regarded as the lingua franca of the scientific world and plays the dominant role in information access and international communication.

However, English was not the dominant language in the beginning. Latin used to be the sole scientific language in Europe, however, researchers started to diverge from it in the 17th century. Newton, Galileo, and others began to write articles in their mother languages partially to make their papers more accessible and partially to respond to the Protestant Reformation and the decaying influence of the Catholic Church. When Latin stopped being the lingua franca, scientific discourse broke into local languages. Because researchers were concerned that the lack of a common language might hinder scientific development, they agreed upon three primary languages by the mid-19th century: French, English and German.

It was not long before Germany held its dominant position before researchers from the U.S., England, France, and Belgium formed prominent scientific organizations after the First World War. They did not accept German scientists due to their reluctance against the previous foes. Another setback struck Germany in 1933, as the authorities fired one-fifth of the country's physics faculty and one-eighth of the biology professors owing to reasons of culture and politics. Many went from Germany to the U.S. and the U.K., where their work began to be published in English.

It took decades for English to become the universal language since the trend started from that point. Due to the Cold War, most scientific articles were published in either English or Russian during the 1950s and 1960s. Then everything changed in the 1970s, for the Soviet Union began to decline, and so did the use of Russian. Around 96 percent of scientific literature throughout the world till the mid-1990s was written in English. Nowadays it is not a choice to publish in English.

Adopting a factual common language of science has had a significant influence on scientific exchanges, which has made it possible for information to be stored and retrieved easily and which might be more efficient than translation and offers a way for knowledge advancement. Researchers can be clear about what to expect and how to search for information thanks to a universal language. So can they be aware of what language to publish in and how to find others' papers that may support their research. In addition to the above-mentioned work, a common language can also ensure that information in presentations, guidelines and standards is accessible to everyone. Only by acquiring a single language can scientists all over the world have access to the enormous scientific literature and so can they communicate with their counterparts throughout the world.

However, there has been controversy regarding the use of English as the universal language, as millions of researchers face a tough and expensive challenge: if they are not native English users, they have to acquire a foreign language alongside their scientific research; Nonetheless, that English is the de facto universal language remains a fact, which is unlikely to change anytime in the near future.

1.3.3 Scientific Writing in English in China

In China, S&T journals are mostly written in Chinese, which prevents them from being read by international academia. The Chinese government had launched the Chinese Science and Technology Journals International Impact Enhancement Program in order to increase the worldwide influence of Chinese academic output. Financial aid, in accordance with the program, is provided by the government to fund new English-language S&T journals published within China so as to enhance China's visibility. At the same time, with the progression of the "Double World-Class project" of China, much importance is placed on international academic output, which paves the way for some high-level universities and disciplines, leading to the top or the front ranks throughout the world by the end of 2050. Admittedly, teaching and learning of English scientific writing in China lays the basis for all these endeavors.

📖 Review Questions

1. What are the differences between academic English and other genres of English?

2. What decides effective academic English?

3. What is the dilemmatic situation of academic writing?

4. Why is English generally regarded as the lingua franca of the international scientific community?

2 Chapter

Genres of Scientific Writing

Learning Objectives

After reading this chapter, you should be able to:

1. Understand the typical features of original research articles, literature review articles, research proposals, conference abstracts and technical reports;

2. Understand the structure and requirements of a thesis and a dissertation.

Chapter Lead-in: Scientists utilize multiple avenues to share their work, including publishing it as an article in a journal, seeking funding for it in the form of a research proposal, or sharing it with a closer group of colleagues through a poster or presentation. This chapter introduces some typical genres of scientific writing, such as research articles, review articles, research proposals, conference proceedings, theses and dissertations, and technical reports.

2.1 Original Research Article

2.1.1 What Is an Original Research Article?

A research article reports the results of original research, assesses its contribution to the body of knowledge in a given area, and is published in a peer-reviewed scholarly journal.

Original research articles are basic sources of scientific literature and deserve an original study. It's necessary for authors to carry out research on a specific topic through experiments, surveys, observation, etc., and present their findings through original research articles. Original research articles, among all the different types of articles published by journals, may be the most valued publications.

A study produces negative results when its findings prove the hypothesis wrong. Note that even though a study does not lead to positive results, it is still original research, helpful learning that can benefit other researchers, and, therefore, publishable. Nevertheless, a publication bias prevails among many peer reviewers and journal editors, who find studies with negative findings less preferable. The scientific community has come to realize that the progress of science can be slowed down if negative results cannot be published. Quite a few journals proactively encourage researchers to publish negative results, countering the publication biases.

An original research article, also called primary scientific literature, will conform to the scientific format, go through peer review and be published in an academic journal. As not everything that satisfies these standards is an original research article, the following features will help tell whether something is an original research article or not.

1) Purpose. An original research article reports original research about new data or theories which have not been published before, such as the results of new experiments, or newly derived models or simulations. In the article, there must be a detailed description of the methods used to produce them so that other researchers can verify them. This description is often presented in a part called "Methods" or "Materials and Methods" or similar. Similarly, the description of the results is usually in great detail, often in a part called "Results".

2) Author. As the original research article reports the results of new research, the authors ought to be the scientists who carried out that research. They will be experts in the field, and will usually work in a university or research lab. In comparison, a newspaper or magazine article will usually be written by a journalist reporting on the actions of someone else.

3) Audience. An original research article will be written by and for scientists working on related topics. As such, accurate technical language should be used in the article to make sure that other researchers can exactly understand what was done, how to do it, and why it matters. Many citations to previous work will also be needed, which may place the research article in a broader context. The article will be published in an academic journal, abide by a scientific format, and go through peer review.

4) Peer review. Scientific research, published in academic journals, goes through a process called "peer review." The peer-review process includes the following steps:
- A paper written by a researcher is sent to an academic journal, where an editor reads it;
- The article is sent by the editor to other scientists with similar expertise, who then evaluate the article;
- Comments or suggestions are made by these scientists;
- These suggestions and comments are given to the original author, who makes changes as needed.

This process repeats till everyone is satisfied and the article can be published in the academic journal.

2.1.2 Format of Original Research Articles

An original research article usually follows the scientific format. A typical original research paper bases the existing research on a topic, discusses a specific question, provides the findings in accordance with a standard structure, and leaves questions for further study and investigation. Among original research of different disciplines, social scientists are particularly interested in controlled investigation and inquiry. Their research often includes observation in the lab or in the field, direct and indirect. Many scientists also write papers to test a hypothesis (i.e., a statement to be tested.)

Although the exact order of research elements may vary more or less due to the specific tasks, most consist of the following elements: Title, Abstract, Introduction, Methods, Results, Discussion, Conclusion, References, Appendix, and so on. Authors typically mark these parts with headings and they may also use subheadings to clarify specific themes within these parts.

1) Title and abstract. The title and abstract have much to do with whether the article will be read or not. Therefore, a title must be descriptive, telling the reader the focus of the study. As many research articles can be accessed via the Internet, a title must contain keywords for an interested reader to find the article. At the same time, the abstract functions as a mini-summary of the study. Many readers will review the abstract, learn about the findings and then decide whether to read the whole article or not.

2) Introduction. The introduction often touches upon the rationale for the paper. What is the phenomenon or event that put you in mind of writing about this topic? How is the topic relevant and why is it significant to study it now? General background must also be presented in your introduction but it should not be a literature review. You only need to give your readers some necessary background information on the history, current circumstances, or other qualities of your topic generally. In other words, what information will a layperson need to know so as to understand the purpose and results of your paper? Finally, give a "road map" to your reader by explaining the general order of the rest of your paper. The road map not only consists of the sections of the following paper, but also includes the main points of each section, some details about your methods, a few main points from your results/analysis, the most essential takeaways from your Discussion section, and the most important conclusion or topic for further study.

3) Literature review. In the literature review, you need to cite key literature which has laid the foundation for this investigation so as to define and identify the state of your topic. In the literature review, you have to clarify relations, contradictions, gaps, and inconsistencies between previous research and this one, and point out the next step in the investigation chain that will be your hypothesis. The review should be written in the present tense as it is ongoing information. The literature review should consist of references, which must be listed in the references part at the end of the article. In comparison with an overview of the previous research, the author(s) can analyze how the study in the article will contribute to and develop the body of knowledge.

4) Methods. This part should sum up the methodology the author(s) used in carrying out the study. It should be written in past tense since the study has already been completed. It must include everything that is necessary to replicate and validate the hypothesis. This section can allow readers to test whether proper research methods have been used to study the question, which also makes it possible for other researchers to replicate the study and see if the same results can be obtained. The challenge in this part lies in knowing the targeted readers well enough to include necessary information without elaborating on "common-knowledge" procedures. Make sure to be specific enough about your research procedure so that others in your field can easily replicate your study. At last, be sure not to report any findings in this part.

5) Results. This part presents the findings from your research. As it is about completed research, it should be written mostly in the past tense. The form and level of detail of the results are determined by the hypothesis and purposes of the report and the needs of the readers. Authors often use visuals in the Results section; however, the visuals should enhance the narrative of the results instead of acting as a substitute. You should develop a narrative based on the themes of the paper and use visuals to convey key findings that deal with your hypothesis or help answer the research question. Include any unexpected results that will clarify the data. It is advisable to use subheadings to organize the Results section according to themes to help the reader learn about the main points or findings of the study. It is easy to mix the Results section with the following Discussion section, in which the author interprets the results of the research. The Results section should only present the results from the data analysis, no matter whether the research is qualitative or quantitative.

6) **Discussion.** The Discussion section interprets the results of the research. The authors usually sum up the findings, evaluate them in the larger context of the existing knowledge, and present the ways in which their findings relate to the prior ones. Any unusual findings will also be discussed in this section. Finally, the authors will report the larger theoretical implications of the findings. This section is for you to report the significance and implications of your study. What is the importance of this study in terms of the hypothesis? In terms of other studies? What are the possible implications for any scientific theories you adopted in the research? Are there any policy implications or suggestions related to the study? Integrate key studies from the literature review into your discussion together with your own data from the Results section. The Discussion section should connect your research with prior study—now you are displaying in a direct way how your finding complements or contradicts other researchers' data and what the broader implications of your results are for experts and the whole society. What questions for future research do these results bring about? As ongoing information, the discussion should be written in the present tense. Sometimes the results and discussion may be combined; in this case, make sure to place equal importance on both.

7) **Conclusion.** Sum up the key results of your study in this final section briefly. This section is not supposed to present new information. You may lay out any limitations from your study design and point out further areas of study or possible projects you would conduct with a new and improved investigatory design.

8) **References.** As citation styles may vary, like APA, MLA, and Chicago, make sure to format the paper and references based on the citation style that your advisor requires or based on the requirements of the scientific journal or conference where you plan to hand in the paper.

9) **Appendix.** The appendix includes attachments that relate to the main document but are too detailed to be included in the main text. These materials must be titled and labeled (for example Appendix A: Questionnaire). You should refer to the appendix in the text with in-text references, and therefore, the reader knows additional useful information is available elsewhere in the document. The following are some examples: regression tables, tables of text analysis data, and interview questions.

2.1.3 General Steps to Structure a Research Article

When organizing your manuscript, you should first know the order of sections will differ a lot from that of items on your checklist. An article starts with the Title, Abstract and Keywords. Its text follows the IMRAD (**I**ntroduction, **M**ethods, **R**esults, **A**nd **D**iscussion) format. The main text is followed by the Conclusion, Acknowledgments, References and Supporting Materials.

Despite the published structure, we usually use a different order when writing, as shown in the following steps:

- Write a clear Conclusion;
- Write a convincing Introduction;
- Write the Abstract;
- Compose a brief and descriptive Title;
- Select Keywords for indexing;
- Write the Acknowledgments;
- Write up the References.

We often finalize the Results and Discussion sections before writing the Introduction section, because, if the Discussion is inadequate, it is difficult for you to present the scientific significance of your work in the Introduction objectively.

Before you begin to write a paper, you should do two important things to build the groundwork for the whole process. The first one lies in the topic to be studied. Identify your hypothesis and goals (these will go in the Introduction). The second one is to review the topic-related literature and choose about 30 papers that can be cited in your paper (these will be listed in the References). Remember that each publisher has its own style guidelines and preferences, so always refer to the publisher's Guide for Authors.

Step 1: Prepare the Figures and Tables

Keep in mind that "a figure is worth a thousand words". Therefore, illustrations, including figures and tables, are the most efficient ways to report your findings. With your data being the driving force of the paper, your illustrations are very important. How do you decide to report your data as tables or figures? In a broad sense, tables show the actual experimental findings, while figures are used to compare experimental results with those of previous works, or with calculated/theoretical values. No matter what you choose, illustrations should not duplicate the information described elsewhere in the manuscript. Another important factor is that figures and tables must be axiomatic, needing no explanation. When presenting your figures and tables, appearances are important. For this purpose:

- Don't use crowded plots, but use only three or four data sets per figure and well-selected scales;

- Consider appropriate axis label size;
- Include clear and easily distinguishable symbols and data sets;
- Avoid long boring tables. They can be included as supplementary material.

Step 2: Write the Methods

This section deals with the question of how the problem was studied. If a new method is proposed in your paper, detailed information must be included for a knowledgeable reader to duplicate the experiment. Whereas, avoid the details of established methods; use References and Supporting Materials to refer to the formerly published procedures. Broad summaries or key references are enough. Incomplete or incorrect methods descriptions will be criticized by reviewers because this section is critical for the reproduction of your research. For this reason, it's vital to adopt standard systems for numbers and nomenclature. Present appropriate control experiments and statistics used, so as to make it possible for the experiment to be repeated. List the methods in the same order as that in the Results section, in the logical order of the study:

- Description of the site;
- Description of the surveys or experiments done, giving information on dates, etc.;
- Description of the lab methods, including separation or treatment of samples, analytical methods;
- Description of the statistical methods used, including confidence levels, etc.

In this section, avoid adding comments, results, and discussion, which is a common error.

Step 3: Write up the Results

This section deals with the question "What did you find?" Hence, you should present only the representative results from your study, which should be essential for discussion. Whereas, keep in mind that most journals provide the possibility of adding Supporting Materials, so use them freely for data of secondary significance. In this case, do not try to "hide" data hoping to save it for a later paper, because you may lose evidence to consolidate your conclusion. If the data is too much, those supplementary materials can be used. Use subheadings to group results of the same type for easier review and reading. Number these subsections for convenient internal cross-referencing. Arrange the data in a logical order to make it clearly presented and easily understandable. Generally, this will be in the same order as reported in the Methods section. Remember not to include references in this section; you are reporting your findings, so you should not refer to others here. If you do so, you are discussing your results, which must be included in the Discussion section.

Step 4: Write the Discussion

Here you need to deal with what the findings mean. It might be the easiest part to write, but the hardest one to get right, because it is the most important section of your article, where you get the opportunity to sell your data. Notice that a large number of manuscripts are turned down due to the weak Discussion. You have to make the Discussion consistent with the Results but not repeat the results. Here you need to compare other published results with yours (using some of the references included in the Introduction). Never overlook work inconsistent with yours, instead, you should confront it and convince the reader you are correct or even better. Consider the following tips:

- Do not make statements beyond what the findings can support;
- Do not use unspecific expressions such as "higher temperature", "at a lower rate", or "highly significant". Use quantitative descriptions instead (30ºC, 0.7%, $p<0.0001$, respectively);
- Avoid abrupt introduction of new terms or ideas; everything must be presented in the Introduction;
- Speculations on possible interpretations can be proposed, which must be rooted in fact, instead of imagination;
- Revision of the Results and Discussion sections is more than paper work, involving further experiments, derivations, or simulations. Sometimes you cannot clarify your idea in words as some critical items have not been studied fully.

Step 5: Write a Clear Conclusion

This section presents how the work develops the field from the current state of knowledge. It can be a separate section in some journals; it can also be the last paragraph of the Discussion section in others. In either case, without a clear Conclusion section, it will be hard for reviewers and readers to evaluate your work and decide if it is publishable in the journal. Repeating the abstract or listing experimental results is the commonly seen error in this section. Trivial statements of your findings are not acceptable in this section. A clear scientific justification for your work must be presented here, indicating uses and extensions if appropriate. Besides, future experiments can be suggested and on going ones can also be pointed out. The current global and specific conclusions related to the objectives can be included in the introduction, as well.

Step 6: Write a Compelling Introduction

This is your chance to let readers believe you know very well why your work is useful. A good introduction responds to the questions below:

- What is the problem to be solved?
- Are there any existing solutions?
- Which is the best?
- What is its main limitation?
- What do you hope to achieve?

The main scientific publications should be introduced, on which your work is based, a few original and important works should be cited, including recent review articles. Nevertheless, editors don't prefer inappropriate citations of too many references impertinent to the work, or improper judgments of your own achievements, because they will deem you have little sense of purpose.

The following are some additional tips for the Introduction:

- Don't use more words than necessary (be brief and to the point). Never make this part into a history lesson, because long introductions bore readers.
- Although you are eager to report your new data, however, remember to present the whole picture at first.
- The introduction must be organized from the global to the specific point of view, leading the readers to your objectives when writing this paper.
- Identify the purpose of the paper and the research strategy adopted to solve the question, but never mix the introduction with results, discussion and conclusion. Always separate them to ensure the logical flow of the manuscript from one section to the next.
- Hypothesis and objectives should be clarified at the end of the introduction.
- Expressions such as "novel", "first time", "first ever" and "paradigm-changing" should be avoided.

Step 7: Write the Abstract

The abstract tells targeted readers about your research and your important findings. Together with the title, the abstract serves as the advertisement of your paper, so make it of interest and easily understood without reading the whole article. Do not use jargon, uncommon abbreviations or references. Accurate words must be used to convey the precise meaning of your study. The abstract gives a short description of the perspective and purpose of your article. It provides key results with little experimental details. Keep in mind that the last sentence of the abstract gives a short description of the interpretation/conclusion. A clear abstract has a strong influence on whether your work will be further considered. Whereas, the abstracts must be kept as concise as possible.

Step 8: Compose a Concise and Descriptive Title

The title explains what the article is mainly about. It is your first (and probably only) chance to capture the reader's attention. In this case, keep in mind that the editor and the referees are the first readers. Meanwhile, the potential authors are also your readers and they will cite your article, so the first impression is critical. Flooded by publications, readers don't have time to read all scientific production, so they have to be selective and often decide whether to read by the title. Reviewers will make sure the title is specific and reflects the content of the manuscript. Editors reject titles that make little sense or represent the subject matter inadequately. Therefore, keep the title informative and concise (clear, descriptive, and not too long) and avoid technical jargon and abbreviations, if possible, because you need to attract as many readers as possible.

Step 9: Select Keywords for Indexing

Keywords, as the label of your paper, are used for indexing your article. Nowadays they are less used by journals as you can search the entire text. Whereas, when pinning down keywords, do not use words with a wide meaning or words of the title. Some journals forbid the keywords to be those from the journal name. For instance, the journal *Soil Biology & Biochemistry* bans the word "soil" from being chosen as a keyword. Only the firmly established abbreviations in the field can be used, rather than those not widely used. Remember to check the Guide for Authors and understand the number of keywords admitted, labels, definitions, thesaurus, range, and other special requests.

Step 10: Write the Acknowledgments

In this section, you can express your gratitude to those who have helped with the manuscript but not to the extent to justify authorship. For instance, here you can include technical assistance with writing and proofreading. Most importantly you should thank your funding agency or the agency offering you a grant or fellowship.

Step 11: Write up the References

There are typically more mistakes in the references than in any other part of the paper, which causes great headaches among editors. Luckily it is now easier to solve these problems thanks to many available tools. In the paper, you should cite all the scientific publications your work is based on. However, do not fill the article with too many references, which doesn't make a better paper. Excessive self-citations must be avoided, and so must too many citations of publications from the same region.

Generally speaking, you ought to use personal communications as few as possible and be aware of how you include unpublished views, which might be necessary for some disciplines, but think of whether they are good or bad for your paper. You may also refer to articles published on research networks before publication, but make sure to balance these citations with those of peer-reviewed studies. When citing research in languages other than English, be mindful that not everyone in the review process can speak the language of the cited paper and so it is helpful to find a translation where possible.

Software, such as EndNote, can help you format and include your references in the article. Make the reference list and the in-text citation strictly according to the style required in the

Guide for Authors. It is the responsibility of the author, not the editor, to present the references in the correct format. Normally, checking the format is a large job for the editors, so they will appreciate the effort if you make their work easier.

2.2　Literature Review Article

2.2.1　What Is a Literature Review Article?

A review article, also called a literature review, is a survey of formerly published material, which attempts to sum up the present state of knowledge on a theme. A review article represents published research from the past, outlines the current understanding of the topic and, different from an original research article, does not report new experimental findings. The purpose of a literature review is to critically evaluate the data available from present studies. Review articles can find out potential study areas for further exploration, which sometimes will reach new conclusions based on the current data.

Review articles come in the form of literature reviews and more specifically, systematic reviews, which are both a form of secondary literature. In literature reviews, the authors summarize what they reckon are the best and most relevant prior publications; in systematic reviews they list objective standards, and select all formerly published original experimental articles that satisfy the standards, and they then compare the results of these articles.

A literature review is mainly designed to summarize and synthesize the ideas from previous papers, without involving personal thoughts or other additional information. Nevertheless, a literature review's objective is to find a central trend or principle presented in all of the publications instead of just listing out summaries of sources.

1. Significance of Literature Reviewing

It is the foundation of all academic research activities, regardless of discipline, to build your research on and relate it to existing knowledge. Therefore, it is a priority for all academics to do so accurately. Whereas, this task has become more and more complex, because knowledge production is increasing at a great speed and meanwhile it is fragmented and interdisciplinary, which makes it difficult to catch up with state-of-the-art research and gain access to the collective evidence in a specific research field. This explains why the literature review is more relevant as a research method than before.

In a broad sense, a literature review can somehow be seen as a systematic method of gathering and synthesizing previous research. As a research way, an effective and well-conducted review creates a solid foundation for knowledge advancement and theory development. With findings and points of view from many empirical findings, a literature review can deal with study questions with a much greater power than any single research.

It can also help present an outline of areas where the research is completely different and interdisciplinary. Additionally, a literature review is a perfect way of synthesizing research findings to provide evidence on a meta-level and to reveal areas where more research is needed, which is a significant component of building theoretical frameworks and creating conceptual models.

Whereas, traditional ways of describing the literature are often not thorough and neither are they undertaken systematically, which leads to a lack of knowledge of what the collection of studies is actually about. Consequently, authors are likely to build their study on flawed assumptions. When researchers use selective evidence for their study, overlooking research that points the other way, serious problems can emerge.

2. Purposes of Literature Reviewing

Conducting a literature review is an approach to displaying an author's knowledge about a specific area of study, including vocabulary, theories, key variables and phenomena, and its methods and history. Conducting a literature review can also let the reader know the important researchers and research groups in the area.

Besides the above reasons for writing a review, there are also many practical reasons for doing so:

- Delineating the research problem;
- Telling what has been done apart from what needs to be done;
- Looking for new lines of inquiry;
- Seeking important variables relevant to the topic;
- Synthesizing and obtaining a new perspective;
- Determining relationships between ideas and practices;
- Building the context of the topic or problem;
- Rationalizing the significance of the problem;
- Enhancing and acquiring the subject vocabulary;
- Understanding the structure of the subject;
- Combining ideas and theory with applications;
- Avoiding fruitless approaches;
- Acquiring methodological insights;
- Discovering the main methodologies and research techniques that have been used;
- Placing the research in a historical setting to seek familiarity with state-of-the-art developments;

- Finding recommendations for further research;
- Seeking support for established theory;
- Providing a framework for relating new findings to previous findings;
- Establishing how the new research develops the previous research.

2.2.2 Format of Literature Review Articles

As with many other kinds of academic writing, a literature review follows a typical introduction-body-conclusion style.

1) Introduction. You should guide your reader(s) toward the MOP (main organizing principle), which means that your information starts from a wide perspective and gradually narrows down until it gets to your focal point. First, present your broad concept. Then narrow your introduction's focus towards the MOP by providing the criteria you used to select the literature sources. Finally, the introduction will end with the presentation of your MOP which should directly link to the sources of literature.

2) Body sections. Generally speaking, each body section will center around a particular source of literature presented in the paper's introduction. Because each source has its own frame of reference for the MOP, it is critical to organize the review in the most logically consistent way possible, which means that the writing should be structured chronologically, thematically, or methodologically.

- Chronologically. Breaking down your sources based on their publication date is a solid way to keep a correct historical timeline. With proper application, it can lay out the development of a certain concept over time and provide examples in the form of literature. Nevertheless, there are sometimes better alternatives to be used to organize the body.
- Thematically. Rather than taking the timeline approach, you can choose another way by looking at the link between your MOP and your sources. Sometimes, the main idea will just glare from a piece of literature. Other times, the author may have to seek out examples to prove their point. An experienced writer will usually present their sources by order of strength.
- Methodologically. As the terminology indicates, this kind of structuring focuses on the methods used to present the central concept. By displaying different methods used to portray the MOP, the writer can compare them based on things like severity, ethicality, and overall impact.

3) Conclusion. After providing your findings in the body sections, you have three final objectives to finish in the article's conclusion. First, the author should summarize the findings they have made or found and briefly answer the question: "What have you learned?" The next step is to report the significance of the information in reference to our present world today.

That is to say, how can the reader take the information and apply it to the current society? From that point, we finish off with a breadcrumb trail. As the author, you want to leave the readers' trail of thought within the actual article topic. This provides them with a way of further investigation—meaning that the reader may think of where the discussion will go next.

2.2.3 General Steps to Write a Review Article

1. Preparing for Your Literature Review

Always remember a literature review gives an all-round overview of relevant publications. Begin by reading literature reviews in journals, and if possible several projects or dissertations handed in by former students to your college. These examples can help you get to know the style and content required, which will give you an idea about how to plan your writing. When reading literature reviews, think of the question of whether the writer is persuasively and logically showing where more research is required. It is crucial to discuss your ideas and the draft questions to study with your supervisors. It is very likely that they may ask questions you cannot answer immediately, but which will help you dig more deeply into your topic. They can help you lay out the main authors and keywords that will focus your online and library literature searches.

It is usually difficult to know where to begin, or indeed what material to use and whether to start with keywords or with authors. A keyword search will find out the academics and the writing important for your research. Keep a list of the keywords and phrases at hand, and add to them as you read, which will help you search the literature in a systematic and logical way.

There are two main strategies for searching—being systematic and snowballing. Using the systematic method, all the papers with a relevant search term in the title or abstract are found. Nevertheless, this approach can lead to long and even unmanageable lists of all possible sources. Snowballing is more organic. Here you select a specific article and build a bibliography of articles to follow up through using the reference list. No matter which method you use (most people combine the two), it is crucial to notice where the paper has been cited and to keep an accurate record. Online searches indicate where a specific article has been cited by later authors.

Once this first stage of searching is completed, the next stage is to read. What follows is a repeated cycle of new reading, which leads you to new authors, new papers and new ideas.

2. Reading for a Literature Review

Read and make notes from many more papers than you actually use because you need to consider the wider evidence so as to choose the relevant items to facilitate your own study. Begin by reading the abstracts, which will help you decide which articles are relevant. In your final report, you may briefly point out study areas that you have thought about and rejected from detailed consideration. The relevant sources may be cited in a short paragraph or table.

For this reading stage, a systematic method such as SQ3R can be useful. This advises you to:

1) Survey. Take your source and re-read the title to make sure it is relevant to your study. Is it a recent article? Scan the introduction and conclusion. If you do not think it is relevant at this point, save it to a separate folder and go on. Note: Do not delete the source, which may become useful later as your study ideas develop.

2) Question. Ask yourself questions about the article. Be conscious about what you are asking, what you already know and what you want to find out from the source. The paper may be relevant for deep and active reading with note-taking, or proper for scan reading to add to present background notes.

3) Read. Be selective. You do not need to read the detailed methodology or every page in a chapter. It is advisable not to take notes the first time you read; it is vital that you recognize the main argument(s) and idea(s). On the next reading, you should take notes and read the detail that you actually need for this specific project.

4) Recall. Reading an article once or twice is not often enough to be certain that you understand what you have read. Take a rest and return to the article, re-read your notes and then try to explain the article in your own words.

5) Review. Having rephrased the content, re-read the article to make sure that you have understood the information without missing anything. Link the sections of your notes with items you have read. Highlight if they support or contradict an opinion.

Although SQ3R may seem long-winded, critical and active reading proves the key to a good literature review. Pay attention to the really important ideas, and you do not need all the details in most cases. As most reviews will cover too much material, it is therefore vital to link one source to another, for instance identifying papers with similar methodologies, outcomes that agree, or results that are contradictory. Mind maps can be useful here. The following tactics may help:

- Copy the reference in full and the library location/online link so you can find it again. This information is needed for your reference list or bibliography.
- Summarize what the article is about in two sentences.
- Summarize the conclusion in one sentence.
- Recognize the strong points of the article and highlight these points in your notes.
- Ask yourself "Is this an argument/case you can agree with?"
- Ask yourself how this information fits in with your present knowledge.
- Ask yourself what you need to know (read) next to develop your understanding of this topic.

After reading, sort your notes into parts for different themes, so that you can easily find them when you write, for which a filing process is needed. Having managed your notes, the next stage is to start to draft your review.

3. Writing Your Literature Review

Writing a literature review is like putting together a jigsaw puzzle. You need to figure out how each piece of writing fits together as well as identify any missing pieces. One common way to approach a literature review is to start out broad and then become more specific. Think of it as an upside-down triangle.

Start by giving a general overview of the broad issues related to your topic or question. You just need to show that you know all the major issues around it. Then narrow your focus to deal with the research and literature that overlap with your topic. Finally, work on any research and literature directly related to your topic, which should take up the largest part of your writing.

After writing your literature review, you may check your work from the following two aspects:

1) Selection of sources:

- Have you stated the reasons for doing your literature review?
- Have you stayed within reasonable boundaries?
- Why did you include some of the literature and exclude others?
- Have you emphasized recent developments?
- Are your sources credible?
- Is the literature you have selected relevant?

2) Critical evaluation of the literature:

- Have you organized your material according to issues?
- Is there a logic to the way you organized the material?
- Does the amount of detail included on an issue relate to its importance?
- Have you been sufficiently critical of design and methodological issues?
- Have you indicated when results were conflicting or inconclusive?
- Have you indicated the relevance of each reference to your research?

2.3 Research Proposal

2.3.1 What Is a Research Proposal?

A research proposal demonstrates what you will study, why it's important, and how you will do the study. Academics often write research proposals to get funding for their projects. As a student, you might need to write it as part of a graduate school application, or you might have to submit one before you start writing your thesis or dissertation. A research proposal is designed to persuade others that you have a relevant and interesting topic to investigate that will yield (in some explicit way) useful outcomes and a plausible idea of how to conduct your study in a timely and economical way. In other words, you must let your target audience believe the project itself is worthwhile and that you are an ideal, capable person to complete it.

The research proposal aims to:

- persuade the reader that your research is interesting, original and important;
- show that you are familiar with the field, you understand the present state of research on the topic, and your views have a strong academic basis;
- make a case for your methodology, showing that you have carefully thought about the data, tools and procedures you will need to conduct the research;
- confirm that the project is feasible within the practical limits of the program, institution or funding.

The length of a research proposal varies greatly, depending on the university, the area of study (e.g., social sciences vs natural sciences), and the level of the degree (e.g., undergraduate, Masters or Ph.D.). A bachelor's or master's thesis proposal may be only several pages, while proposals for Ph.D. dissertations and research funding are often very long and detailed. In some cases, a rough outline of the topic is what's needed, while in other cases, universities ask for a very detailed proposal that forms the first three chapters of the dissertation or thesis. So, it's always best to check with your university what their specific requests are before you get on with your proposal.

1. Types of Research Proposals

There are different types of research proposals, which may be classified as follows:

1) Solicited proposals. These are proposals submitted in response to a specific call issued by a sponsor. Such solicitations, typically called Request for Proposals (RFP), or Request for Quotations (RFQ), usually have specific requirements for format and technical content and may specify certain award terms and conditions.

2) Unsolicited proposals. These are proposals submitted to a sponsor who has not issued a particular solicitation but is believed by the researcher to be interested in the subject.

3) Pre-proposals. These are requested by a sponsor who wants to minimize an applicant's effort in preparing a full proposal. Pre-proposals are usually in the form of a letter of intent or a brief abstract. After the pre-proposal is reviewed, the sponsor lets the researcher know if a full proposal is warranted.

4) Continuation or non-competing proposals. These confirm the original proposal and funding requirements of a multi-year project for which the sponsor has already provided funding for an initial period (normally one year). Continued support usually depends on satisfactory work progress and the availability of funds.

5) Renewal or competing proposals. Proposals that require continued support for an existing project that is about to end. These requests—in the sponsor's eyes—generally have the same status as an unsolicited proposal.

2. Dissertation/Thesis Research Proposals

A dissertation/thesis research proposal is a structured, formal document which demonstrates what you plan to study (i.e., your research topic), why it's worth studying (i.e., your justification), and how you plan to investigate it (i.e., your practical approach). The purpose of the research proposal is to convince your research advisor, committee or university that your investigation fits the requirements of the degree program and is manageable despite the time and resource limits you will face.

The most important word here is "convince"—that is to say, your research proposal has to sell your research idea to whoever is going to approve of it. If it fails to convince him or her of its suitability and manageability, you'll have to revise and resubmit, which will cost you precious time, which will either delay the start of your research or waste its time allowance.

A good dissertation or thesis proposal needs to cover the "what", the "why" and the "how" of the research.

1) What: Your research topic. Your proposal needs to voice your research topic, specifically and unambiguously. Your research topic should exactly articulate what you plan to research and in what context. So, remember that your research proposal gives a detailed explanation of your research topic. Never start writing your proposal until you have a crystal-clear topic in mind, or you'll end up writing down a few thousand useless words.

2) Why: Your justification. It's not good enough to just propose a research topic—you also need to demonstrate why your topic is original. In other words, what makes it unique? What gap in the present literature does it fill? If it's simply a restatement of the existing study, it will hardly be approved of—it needs to be fresh. But, originality alone is not enough. Once you've met that criterion, you also need to justify why your proposed topic matters. In other words, what value will it bring to the world if you succeed in answering your research questions? So, when you're writing your research proposal, keep in mind that it's not enough for a topic to be unique. It needs to be useful and value-creating, which must be conveyed in your proposal.

3) How: Your methodology. It's good to have an original and important topic, however, you cannot gain approval without analyzing the practicalities—in other words: How will you conduct your research? Is your research design proper for your topic? Is your plan feasible given your limits (time, money, expertise)?

During the proposal stage, you do not have a fully mapped-out research strategy, nevertheless, you have to provide a high-level view of your research methodology and some major design decisions. The following are some vital questions you'll need to answer in your proposal: Will you take a qualitative or quantitative approach? Will your design be cross-sectional or longitudinal? How will you collect your data (interviews, surveys, etc.)? How will you analyze your data (e.g., statistical analysis, qualitative data analysis, etc.)? So, be clear you think about the practicalities of your research and have at least a basic understanding of research methodologies before you begin drafting your proposal.

2.3.2　Format of Research Proposals

The format of a research proposal varies from field to field, but most proposals share some common elements. Proposals for sponsored activities usually contain a similar format; variations depend on whether the proposer is applying for a research grant, a training grant, or a conference or curriculum development project. The following outline includes the primary parts of a research proposal.

1. Title Page

The format for the title page is specified by most sponsoring agencies, and special forms are provided with basic administrative and fiscal data for the project. Titles ought to be brief but comprehensive enough to signify the nature of the proposed work.

2. Abstract

The funder may, according to the abstract, make preliminary decisions about the proposal. Thus, a successful summary presents the problem dealt with by the applicant, states the solution, clarifies the objectives and methods of the project, outlines funding requirements and describes the applicant's competence.

3. Table of Contents

A table of contents is not needed for brief proposals with few sections. However, long and detailed proposals may require not only a table of contents but a list of illustrations (or figures) and a list of tables. If all of these sections are included, they must follow the above order, and each should be numbered with lower-case Roman numerals. The table of contents lists all main sections and divisions, with the abstract included.

4. Introduction

The introduction (including Statement of Problem, Purpose of Research, and Significance of Research) of a proposal begins with a brief statement and then moves on to introduce the subject to a stranger. Sufficient background must be provided to make sure an informed layperson can put your specific research problem in the context of common knowledge. The introduction also indicates how its solution will develop the area or be significant for some other work. The statement portrays the significance of the problem(s) about proper studies or statistics.

Some crucial questions to guide your introduction include: Who is interested in the topic (e.g., scientists, practitioners, policymakers, particular members of society)? How much is already known about the problem? What is missing from present knowledge? What new perspectives will your research contribute? Why is this research worth doing?

5. Literature Review

In this section, you need to make sure to:

- Be clear about what the research problem is and exactly what has been accomplished;
- Provide proof of your ability in the area;
- Explain why the previous work needs to be further studied.

An effective literature review makes the reader believe that your project has a strong foundation in current knowledge or theory. It also demonstrates that you're not just repeating what other people have already done or said. The literature review should be selective and critical. Discussions of others' previous work are supposed to convince the reader how you will proceed with the past study and also how your work is different from theirs.

In this section, you should aim to show exactly how your project will make contributions to dialogs in the area. You may use the following techniques:

- Compare and contrast: What are the main theories, methods, debates and controversies?
- Be critical: What are the strengths and weaknesses of different methods?
- Demonstrate how your study fits in: How will you build on, challenge, or integrate others' work?

6. Description of Proposed Research (Including Method or Approach)

Other specialists in your field are readers of the all-directional explanation of the proposed research. This section is the core of the proposal and is the primary concern of the technical reviewers. Keep in mind as you lay out the research design to:

- Be realistic about what can be achieved;
- Be clear about any assumptions or hypotheses the research method depends on;
- Be explicit about the focus of the research;
- Be as detailed as possible about the timeline of the proposed research;
- Be specific about the methods of evaluating the data or the conclusions;
- Be sure there is an evident connection between the research objectives and the research approach;

- Clarify preliminary work developing an analytical approach or laying the groundwork as Phase 1;
- Report that you have accomplished something and are ready to start Phase 2.

The Research Design or Methodology section should explain the comprehensive method and practical procedures you will take to study your research questions. Do not simply write a list of methods. Aim to convince readers why this is the most proper, valid and reliable approach to answering your questions.

7. Implications and Contribution to Knowledge

To complete your proposal on a powerful note, you can explore the hidden implications of the research for theory or practice, and stress again what you aim to contribute to the present knowledge on the topic. For instance, your findings may have implications for: improving processes in a particular location or field; informing policy objectives; enhancing a theory or model; questioning popular or scientific assumptions; building a basis for further investigation.

8. Description of Relevant Institutional Resources

Generally, this section gives detailed information on the resources available to the proposed project and if possible, indicates why the sponsor should choose this institution and this researcher for this specific study. Here are some relevant points:
- The institution's demonstrated skill in the related research field;
- Its abundance of experts in related areas that may indirectly help the project;
- Its supportive services that will directly benefit the project;
- Its unique or special research facilities or resources available to the project.

9. Reference List or Bibliography

Your research proposal should include appropriate citations for all sources you have used, and full publication details can never be missing from the reference list. You might be, in some cases, required to include a bibliography, which is a list of every source you consulted in preparing the proposal, even ones you did not cite in the text, and sometimes also other relevant sources that you plan to read. The aim is to portray the full range of literature that will support your research project. The style of the bibliographical item depends on the disciplinary field. You should mainly consider consistency; in other words, whatever style is chosen should be followed carefully throughout the entire proposal.

10. Research Schedule

In some cases, you might have to include a detailed schedule of the project, stating exactly what you will do at each phase and how long it will take. Check the requirements of your program or funding body to see if this is required.

11. Personnel

This section is usually composed of two parts: an explanation of the proposed personnel arrangements, and the biographical data sheets for each of the major contributors to the project. The explanation should make it clear how many persons at what percentage of time and in what academic categories will be taking part in the program. If the project is complex and involves people from other departments or colleges, specify the organization of the staff and the lines of responsibility. Any student participation, paid or unpaid, should be mentioned, and the nature of the proposed contribution detailed. If any persons must be hired for the program, say so, and explain why, unless the need for persons not already available within the institution is self-evident.

12. Budget

If you are applying for research funding, you will probably also have to include a detailed budget that indicates how much each section of the project will cost. Remember to check what kind of costs the funding body will approve of, and then only cover relevant items in your budget. Each item may include:

- Cost: Exactly how much money do you need?
- Justification: Why is this cost necessary to complete the research?
- Source: How did you calculate the amount?

13. Revisions and Proofreading

Like in other academic writing, it's indispensable to redraft, edit and proofread your research proposal before you hand it in. If you have the opportunity, ask a supervisor or colleague for feedback. For the best chance of approval, you are advised to use a professional proofreading service to eliminate language errors, check your proposal's structure, and improve your academic style.

2.4 Conference Abstract

2.4.1 What Is a Conference Abstract?

Learning how to write an abstract for a conference is a critical skill for early-career researchers. The purpose of an abstract is to summarize the major aspects of the paper you want to present, so you must learn to write a complete but concise abstract that does your conference paper justice. Your conference abstract is often the only piece of your work that conference organizers will see, so it needs to be strong enough to stand alone. And once your work is accepted or published, researchers will only consider attending your presentation or reading the rest of your paper if your abstract compels them to. So learning how to write an abstract well is pretty important. Happily, while every research discipline varies, most successful abstracts follow a similar formula.

A conference abstract is a short document, designed to attract the interest of a possible reader of your article. Therefore, it is kind of a marketing document for your entire article. If the abstract is poorly written or boring, then it cannot encourage a potential reader to read your full paper. Hence the first rule of conference abstract writing is that it should capture the reader's attention by telling him or her what your paper is about and why he or she should read it.

In the body of the conference abstract, you need to clearly state the topic of your paper and your research question. You need to say how your research was/is being conducted. For instance, is it empirical or theoretical? Is it quantitative or qualitative? What value do your results have and to whom will they be useful? The conference abstract should then concisely portray the work to be discussed in your paper and also briefly summarize the findings. Finally, your conference abstract should not include diagrams and references that are usually not required. It needs to be written within a certain word limit set by the conference committee, typically 300–350 words.

2.4.2 Format of a Conference Abstract

1. Formula for Writing an Abstract

When drafting a conference abstract, you are advised to follow this formula for success: topic + title + motivation + problem statement + approach + results + conclusions = conference abstract. Here's a more detailed formula. You may adapt it to fit your research discipline.

1) Abstract topic. How will your abstract convince the conference organizers that you'll add to the conversations on a specific topic at their event? Your conference presentation will have a limited scope, so select a perspective that fits the conference topics and plan your abstract through that lens.

2) Abstract title. What is your conference paper about and what makes it interesting? Normally give your abstract a title of 12 words or less.

3) Motivation. Why should your readers care about the problem and your results? This part should present the background to your study, the significance of it, and the difficulty of the area.

4) The problem. What problem are you addressing? Are you using a generalized method, or is it for a particular situation? (If the problem your research tries to answer is widely recognized, include this section before motivation.) Make a clear statement of the topic of your paper and your research question in this part.

5) Study design. What was your approach to solving the problem or making progress on it? How did you design your study? What was the extent of your research?

6) Predictions and results. What results or trends did your analysis uncover? Were they as you expected or not?

7) Conclusions. What do your findings mean? How will they contribute to your field? Will they shake things up, speed things up, or simply show other researchers that this particular area may be a dead end? Are your results general or highly specific?

2. Tips for Writing a Successful Conference Abstract

Because conference organizers usually have more submissions than presentation slots, you may use these tips to increase the chances for your abstract to be successful.

1) Carefully select your abstract keywords. Abstract keywords help your work to be found by other researchers when it's published, and lots of conferences request that authors submit papers with keywords, which should be the words that most precisely reflect the content of your paper.

2) Find example abstracts. Familiarize yourself with different conference abstracts. Gain access to the conference book of abstracts from previous years—if you can't find it online, your advisor may have a copy lying about. Look for examples of abstracts handed in by early-career researchers, and try to figure out what made each one successful.

3) Edit with fresh eyes. After you've written your abstract, stay away from it for at least a day. Revising it with fresh eyes can help you be more objective in deciding what's vital.

4) Cut filler and jargon. Because of limited space, you must be as concise as possible by cutting unnecessary words or phrases. Keep sentences short enough so that you can read them aloud without having to pause for breath. And avoid jargon, specific to one field, especially when you're handing in to an interdisciplinary conference.

5) Submit early. Conference organizers usually start reviewing abstracts ahead of the submission deadline, and they're often swamped with submissions right before the deadline. Hand in your abstract well before the deadline and you may get a bigger chance to be accepted.

6) Submit often. As an early-career researcher, conferences are often the first place you'll have your work published, so conference abstracts are an ideal place to learn. The more abstracts you write and hand in, the better you'll be at writing them. So never give up trying.

2.5

Thesis and Dissertation

2.5.1 What Is a Thesis/Dissertation?

As a college student, you will face various challenging coursework and assignments. Whereas, your thesis or dissertation will be the biggest project for you to work on when getting your master's or doctoral degree.

A thesis is a critically written academic piece of research work. Typically, it is handed in by students completing a master's program. The purpose of it is to allow students to demonstrate their knowledge and expertise within the subject matter they have been learning as part of the master's degree. A dissertation is a relatively longer piece of scholarly writing that reflects your research work in the entire doctoral program. A researcher earns the Ph.D. after handing in and defending his or her dissertation, which consists of all information about the original research or expanded research on a new or existing topic by the Ph.D. candidate.

There are plenty of differences between a dissertation and a thesis because they happen at different times in one's educational journey. A thesis and a dissertation primarily differ in the time of their completion. As mentioned earlier, the former is presented at the culmination of a master's program, nevertheless, the latter is presented to earn a Ph.D. A thesis is a compilation of research indicating that the researcher has gained information about the research topic learned in the study program. Whereas, a dissertation offers a chance for the researcher to contribute new theories and knowledge to the present literature in the research area. A thesis presents acquired and existing information, on the other hand, a dissertation aims to propose a unique concept and defend it on the basis of theoretical and practical findings.

A master's thesis is roughly 100 pages in length. Nevertheless, a Ph.D. dissertation is much lengthier with background and research information. A dissertation must include your research proposal, grant proposal, literature review, ideation of research topic, and all other minute details about your research. A dissertation ideally should be three times as long as a master's thesis.

Also, there are plenty of similarities between a dissertation and a thesis, as shown in the following:

- Both a thesis and a dissertation are regarded as a final project and required to graduate from different programs;
- Both thesis and dissertation require profound and accurate knowledge of the research problem;

- Both forms of academic written pieces must deal with particular research questions;
- Scholarly writing skills are indispensable for a thesis and a dissertation;
- Ethical practices must be followed while checking and documenting research data;
- Plagiarism is banned in either;
- Analytical skills are required in both to support the results;
- Both require intense editing and critical proofreading before final submission.

Interestingly, the definitions of a thesis and a dissertation are almost opposite from each other in Europe and the United States. In Europe, the original difference between a thesis and a dissertation has been largely kept. A doctoral thesis is a focused piece of original research that is conducted to earn a Ph.D. A dissertation is part of a wider post-graduate research project. Nevertheless, the thesis has developed as nowadays original research needs lots of background research. Therefore, a thesis will contain broader citations and references to earlier work, despite the focus on the original work that comes out of it. In the United States, the definition of a thesis is almost the opposite of that in Europe. Because a thesis is shorter than a dissertation, it gradually came to mean a preliminary degree on the way to a doctorate. A thesis is now written for a master's degree. In scientific areas, a master's candidate has advanced course work and gets first-hand experience in a research project without directing the project to the same extent that he would in a doctoral program. In a master's project, the student's ideas are encouraged but the focus is on gaining technical expertise, not doing original research. Engineering students usually obtain master's degrees and seldom pursue Ph.D.s. In other disciplines such as chemistry, the opposite is true.

Evidently, the dissertation vs. thesis facts are real. Therefore, it is unacceptable to use one term instead of another as an academic. One must remember the purpose of each and use them accurately. Whereas, one is not undermined by the other. Whether you are writing a thesis or a dissertation, you must perform with the same seriousness, critical technical and soft skills. Improved time management and better academic writing skills can help you ace both forms of academic writing.

2.5.2 Structure and Requirements of Theses and Dissertations

In form, a thesis (the same as a dissertation) features a problem-method-results-discussion structure and is a long experimental, design or theoretical report. This recurring hypothetic-deductive pattern of developing a thesis to solve a problem and then building a methodology and testing for results is common in research writing. When drafting a thesis, you need to structurally consider the front matter, the body, and the end matter as shown in the following.

1. Front Matter

The front matter frames the thesis work, including the following elements:

1) Title page. You are supposed to follow a standard title page form of your department. The title must be informative, include keywords, and unfold the topic of the thesis. Contain the title, author, thesis supervisor, place, and date.

2) Abstract. You are expected to concisely state the research problem, methodology, key results, and conclusion.

3) Table of contents. List the key subject headings and subheadings of your thesis with their page numbers. Number the front-matter section in lowercase Roman numerals. Remember to include acknowledgments, appendixes, and bibliography.

4) List of figures. Include the figure numbers, figure titles, and page numbers.

5) List of tables. Include the table numbers, table titles, and page numbers.

6) Nomenclature (optional). List unfamiliar terms, symbols, acronyms and their meanings.

2. Body

In the thesis body, you present the introduction, narrative and analysis of your work, including the following elements:

1) Introduction. State the purpose of the study, the problem being studied, the background (context and significance) of the problem (citing previous work by others), your thesis statement and general method, and the standards for your study's success.

2) Theory. Build the theoretical basis for your design or experimental work, including any governing equations. Detailed calculations go to an appendix.

3) Materials, apparatus, and procedures. List and describe key materials and apparatus. Then describe the procedure in a detailed way so that others can reproduce it. The section of design studies consists of component design, fabrication, assembly, and testing procedures. Use illustrations.

4) Results. Report the results, usually with accompanying tables and graphs. Characterize the patterns and quality of the results and estimate their accuracy and precision. Detailed data are included in an appendix. Use analytical graphics.

5) Discussion. Make discussions of the meaning of the results, and make a clear statement of what their importance is. Compare the results with theoretical expectations and explain anything unexpected.

6) Conclusions. Go over the results about the original problem statement. Evaluate the success of the study according to the standards of success you provided in the introduction.

7) Recommendations. If applicable, recommend directions for future work.

3. End Matter

The end matter is mainly referential material too detailed to fit in the main narrative of work done, including the following elements:

1) Acknowledgments. Acknowledge assistance from advisors, sponsors, funding agencies, colleagues, technicians, etc.

2) Appendixes. List detailed calculations, procedures and data in separate appendixes. Each appendix should have a title, a letter (Appendix A, B, C), and an introductory paragraph.

3) Bibliography. List alphabetically any works involved in your study. Follow the bibliographical and footnote formats of your department or a prominent periodical published by a professional organization in your field.

Research is a vital component of graduate education. The thesis or dissertation is often considered to be the culmination of graduate work as well as the formal product. Nevertheless, the process requires the efforts of many people. The two essential parts of this work are the major advisor and advisory committee, which interact with a master's or doctoral student, create an important professional experience and influence the degree work and resulting thesis or dissertation. The communication between the major advisor and the student is one of the most significant aspects of graduate work. Various approaches, circumstances, and personalities can make communication difficult. After all, it is the student's responsibility to complete his or her thesis or dissertation and to create work of superior quality.

2.6 Technical Report

2.6.1 What Is a Technical Report?

A technical report is a common document describing the process and results of technical or scientific research. It may include in-depth experimental details, data, and further research recommendations. Technical reports are usually written to report on a specific research problem/question. All the technical information must be presented in a clear and easily accessible format. It must be divided into sections that allow readers to access different types of information.

Usually, technical reports aren't peer-reviewed but are evaluated mostly on how the problem, research methods, and results are described. If the data is to the point, there won't be any problem. Moreover, if it is formatted properly, it will be highly appreciated. In general, technical report writing is a means of allocating and summarizing knowledge that is gained through the observation of a certain process, experiment, or phenomenon. To write a technical report, the writer has to bear a clear and objectified understanding of the subject matter. It is important to be meticulous and record as many details as possible when studying the problem.

Technical reports are important for the following reasons:

1) Efficient communication. Technical reports are used by industries to report relevant information to upper management, who will make critical decisions based on the information. Such technical reports include proposals, regulations, manuals, procedures, requests, progress reports, emails, and memos.

2) Evidence for your work. Most of the technical work is backed by software. Nevertheless, graduation projects are not. So, if you're a student, your technical report, as the sole evidence of your work, shows the steps you took for the study and justifies your efforts for a better assessment.

3) Organizing the data. A technical report, as a brief, factual piece of information, conforms to a standard manner. It is the one place where all the data of a project is written in a condensed way that is easily comprehensible by a reader.

4) Tool for evaluation of your work. Your research project is mainly assessed by professors and supervisors according to the technical write-up for it. With a precise, clear, and understandable report, you will certainly gain a good grade.

When writing a technical report, you should adopt the following writing style:

- Avoid using slang or informal words. For example, use "cannot" instead of "can't".
- Use a third-person tone and avoid using words like "I" or "me".
- Each sentence should be grammatically complete with an object and subject.
- Two sentences should not be linked via a comma.
- Avoid the use of passive voice.
- Tenses should be carefully employed. Use present for something that is still viable and past for something no longer applicable.
- Always think of readers while writing. Avoid giving them instructions. Your work is to make their work of evaluation easier.
- Abbreviations should be avoided and if used, the full form should be mentioned.
- Understand the difference between a numbered list and a bulleted list. Numbering is used when something is explained sequence-wise, whereas bullets are used to just list out points where the sequence is not important.
- All the preliminary pages (title, abstract, preface..) should be named in small Roman numerals (i, ii, iv...).
- All the other pages should be named in Arabic numerals (1, 2, 3...), hence your report starts with 1—on the introduction page.

- Separate long texts into small paragraphs to keep the reader engaged. A paragraph should not be more than 10 lines.
- Do not incorporate too many fonts. Use standard Times New Roman 12pt for the text. You can use bold for headlines.

2.6.2 Typical Structure of Technical Reports

When writing a technical report, you can follow two approaches, depending on what is more suitable. First, top-down approach. In this, you organize the whole report from title to subsections and conclusion and then start putting in the matter in the respective chapters, which gives your thought a defined flow and thus helps in time management, too. Second, evolutionary delivery. This approach suits you if you believe in "going with the flow". Here you may write and decide as and when the work develops, which gives you a wide thinking horizon. You can even add and edit some parts when you have a new idea or inspiration.

A technical report features a defined structure that is easy to navigate and clearly describes the objective of the report. Your technical report should have this list of pages, set in the order.

1) Cover page. As the face of your project, it must include details like the title, name of the author, and name of the institution with its logo. The cover page should be simple but eye-catching.

2) Title page. Apart from all the information on the cover page, the title page also tells the reader about the status of the project, for example, technical report part 1, final report, etc. This page also mentions the name of the mentor or supervisor.

3) Abstract. In a technical report, an abstract briefly sums up the report, including what the subject matter is and what the main research results and conclusions are. It is also called the executive summary, which offers a concise and explicit overview of the project. In other words, a person only reading the abstract can have complete information on the project.

4) Preface. It is an announcement page in which you claim that you have given due credit to all the sources and that no part of your research is plagiarized. The results are of your experiment and study.

5) Dedication. On this optional page, authors can dedicate their study to loved ones. It is a small sentence in the middle of a new page, which is mainly used in theses.

6) Acknowledgment. Here, you convey acknowledgment to the people, parties, and institutions who assisted you in the process or enlightened you on the idea of it.

7) Table of contents. The table of contents, as the name means, lists everything in the report. All the main parts of the report must be listed with page numbers for easy navigation. In addition, second/third-level headings can be listed for a more detailed table of contents.If symbols have been used, then a similar nomenclature page is also made. Also, if a lot of graphs and tables have been included, a separate content page for that needs to be created. Each of these lists begins on a new page.

8) Introduction. An introduction is a section stating the objectives of writing the report and some extra information on how the topic is covered in the report. On this page, you should explicitly clarify the context of the report, by identifying the purpose of the project, and the questions you have answered in your report. And sometimes you may also provide an overview of the report. Remember that your conclusion must answer the objective questions. The introduction should put forward the significance of the study being reported. You must not include too much background information on the topic; instead, try to be as specific as you can.

9) Central sections. The body of the report consists of these numbered and headed parts—methods, materials, analysis procedure, findings, discussion, and solutions, which makes it easier for the reader to understand what you are discussing in your report. All these sections/chapters logically specify the main ideas of a step-by-step analysis of any given problem/phenomenon.

10) Conclusion. The conclusion summarizes the major ideas drawn from the report based on the importance of the results reported. Note that readers often read conclusions first without paying attention to the entire report. The final phrases always matter because they are supposed to give the answers provided by a research or test.

11) Appendices. Appendices (if appropriate) include information that can support your report, such as tables, diagrams, etc. This extra information from the appendix doesn't have to be explained in detail in the report, however, this section should directly relate to the studied problem or the report's objective. Items in the appendices should be listed in the same order as in the research.

12) References/Bibliography. References include the actual material you refer to in your research, previously published by someone else, while a bibliography takes account of all the data you read, got inspired from, or gained knowledge from, which does not need to be a direct part of your investigation. The reference list or bibliography is a very crucial part of your report, as it proves your evidence strongly, which can convince the reader that you refer to some sources of information during your research for the report, by citing the sources which the information has been taken from, such as figures, statistics, graphs, or word-to-word sentences. You may face a legal threat without this part. In this section, due credit must be given to the sources and so must your support be shown to other people who have worked on the same area.

Review Questions

1. What is an original research article?

2. What is a literature review article?

3. What is a research proposal?

4. What is a conference abstract?

5. What is a thesis? What is a dissertation?

6. What are the structures and requirements of a thesis and a dissertation, respectively?

7. What is a technical report?

3 Chapter

Process of Scientific Writing

Learning Objectives

After reading this chapter, you should be able to:

1. Understand research topic, research question and research title;
2. Understand the reasons for and the ways of choosing a research topic;
3. Understand literature searching and reviewing;
4. Understand the strategies for drafting;
5. Understand the steps and techniques for revising;
6. Understand proofreading.

Chapter Lead-in: Writing can be intimidating, even if you are an experienced writer. But breaking writing down into simpler steps can help you write faster and better. The writing process refers to the steps someone takes to compose a text. There are basic writing process steps that are universally referred to and followed. Following a proper writing process is important for a few good reasons. By breaking down the task into manageable steps, you can do away with struggling and procrastinating. Since you will be following individual steps, you can focus on each step better, which in turn will be reflected in the quality of the final copy. There are many different processes for writing, such as three steps (i.e., planning, writing, completing), four steps (i.e., pre-writing, writing, revising, editing), five steps (i.e., brainstorming, preparing/research, drafting, revising, proofreading/publishing), six steps (i.e., pre-writing, drafting, revising, editing, publishing, marketing/reflecting) and even seven steps (i.e., planning, drafting, sharing, evaluating, revising, editing, publishing). This chapter introduces the scientific writing process as a seven-step one: topic choosing and selecting, literature searching and reviewing, outlining, drafting, revising, proofreading and publishing.

3.1 Topic Choosing and Selecting

3.1.1 Research Topic, Research Question and Research Title

1. Research Topic

A research topic is a subject or an issue that a researcher shows interest in when carrying out research. A well-defined research topic paves the way for successful research. A well-chosen topic takes researchers plenty of time to dig, define, and develop their ideas. A good research topic is something that one shows great interest in, is scientifically original and important, and is feasible within the time frame. Specificity determines all the qualities of a good research topic. In other words, every research topic must specifically answer a research question.

There are some basic criteria to decide whether a research topic is right for a thesis, dissertation, or any other scientific research. A good research topic should have these qualities:

1) Clear. Clarity is the most important quality of any research topic. The topic must be clear enough so that people can easily understand the nature of the research. The research topic should have a single interpretation and must be free of any ambiguity so that others cannot be misled. Clarity also means that the research topic must be directional, which sets the whole research methodology.

2) Well-defined and well-phrased. Well-defined and well-phrased research topic builds the foundation for a successful research. To be easily understood, the research topic should be well-defined and well-phrased, with a single meaning. When the research topic is not well-defined, the researcher can't create the right objectives and the hypothesis, which may worsen as the research goes on. Simple language must be used in the research topic and technical terms shall be avoided unless it is necessary. Never introduce, in the research topic, any kind of bias directly or indirectly, willingly or unwillingly.

3) Of current importance. The current importance of a research topic must be given serious consideration because an obsolete topic will not be beneficial for anyone. How much benefit the topic will contribute to the research area should be evaluated during the consideration.

2. Research Question

A research question is vital to the research process, as the research is centered around it. Research questions keep writers focused on their study by blazing a trail through the investigation and writing process. The specificity of a well-developed research question prevents writers from composing the "all-about" paper and leads them toward a specific, arguable thesis. A research question should be:

1) Clear. Research questions must be as clear as possible to help the writer direct his or her research with enough specifics that help the audience easily understand its purpose while needing no additional explanation.

2) Focused. Research questions must be narrow and specific enough to be well covered in the space the writing task allows.

3) Complex. Research questions should not be answerable with a simple "yes" or "no" or by easily found facts. Instead, they require both research and analysis of ideas and sources before the composition of an answer, which often begins with "how" or "why".

4) Arguable. Its potential answers are open to debate instead of accepted facts.

3. Research Title

The title sums up the main idea or ideas of a study. The initial aim of a title is to attract the reader's attention and to draw it to the research question being studied. A good title consists of the fewest possible words that adequately portray the contents and/or purpose of a research paper. Undoubtedly, the title is the most read part of a paper, and it is the first read part in most cases.

Upon necessity, a more detailed classification of the research title may be involved, i.e., working title, final title and subtitle. Typically, the final title is formulated after the research is ended so that the title precisely describes what was done. The working title should be decided early to help navigate the focus of the research in the same way the research problem does.

Reviewing the working title can help return to the main objective of the research if the writing is felt being tangent.

Successful titles in scholarly research papers have these attributes:

- Identify the subject and scope of the research accurately;
- Avoid using abbreviations;
- Use words that bring a positive impression and capture the reader's interest;
- Use present nomenclature from the field of research;
- Specify key variables, both dependent and independent;
- Indicate how the paper will be organized;
- Suggest a relationship between variables that supports the major hypothesis;
- Is limited to 10 to 15 substantive words;
- Do not contain "study of", "analysis of" or similar constructions;
- Is usually in the form of a phrase, but can also be in the form of a question;
- Is seldom followed by an exclamation mark.

Subtitles are quite common in social sciences research papers. Subtitles may:

- explain or provide additional context;
- add substance to a literary, provocative or imaginative title;
- qualify the geographic scope of the research;
- qualify the temporal scope of the research;
- focus on studying the ideas, theories or work of a specific individual;
- specify the methodology used;
- define the principal technique for analyzing the research problem.

3.1.2 How to Choose a Research Topic

The first step of a research paper is to choose a topic. Considering the backgrounds of those topics may help you choose one. Ponder over why such topics capture your interest and what has inspired you to go down those paths. Think about how such ideas have evolved and progressed over time and why they are most outstanding. Doing this will help you fully understand what you want to focus on at a given time.

Your motivation for getting some topic to work for you can make a difference. The motivation makes it necessary for you to think about what interests you the most about a topic and whether that topic is sensible to your interests. You should look at how much information you want to get out of that topic and what points interest you about that topic more than anything else, which could provide you with more help for writing a paper without being too complicated or difficult to follow.

When thinking about the things you can do, you have to look at the resources available. Topics are sometimes chosen based on the resources which can be utilized. It is best to think about how such resources are organized and how up-to-date they are. Anything that branches off into many aspects of a topic of value can help. No matter what the case is, the content should be understandable and easy to follow.

You must also consider your research topic based on how complicated or otherwise hard it might be. You can always work on a good topic that has enough information in it to where it won't be too difficult to follow. You have to know what you're doing when selecting an ideal topic for your research. You will be sticking with that research topic for a long time so make sure that the research paper topic you pick is something that you know you can stand behind.

1. Procedures for Choosing a Research Topic

It can be challenging to write a paper, however, choosing a topic can be even more daunting. You may have difficulty figuring out where to start or whether your area will provide sufficient resources for a thesis. Brainstorming ideas, performing preliminary research, and refining your general idea can help choose an effective paper topic that you'll be excited and prepared to write about.

1) Brainstorming research topics. Brainstorming is usually an effective way for students to write some ideas down on paper. Putting one's ideas down often gives momentum to the writing process. Though brainstorming works particularly well when a topic has been selected, it can also help you narrow a topic. In this writing period, you write down—often in list or bulleted form—all ideas that occur to you. At the end of the session, you can examine your list for consistent patterns. If something appears to be more prominent in your mind than others, it might be a possible topic.

Note that the original topic you put forward may not be the one that you write about, because your ongoing research determines the research topics, which are usually fluid. Such fluidity is common in research, and you should accept it as one of its many features.

Make sure whether the paper needs a particular focus. If you are designated a topic, you should meticulously follow the instructions given by your professor. If there is a range of topics for you to choose from, think of which interests you most. Some preliminary research on several topics may also help you see which has the most information available.

Do a timed writing session to formulate a list. After flashing the recent work in your mind, take a pencil and paper to jog down a list. Set a timer for five minutes and put down as many topics as you can think of within that time. Don't be too picky of yourself in this early phase; the purpose is to get some ideas out. Your brain may make unexpected and pleasant connections, which don't have to be firm thesis statements. Just build a base of ideas.

Look for patterns or areas of interest. Peruse your list and use symbols, such as stars or asterisks, to mark related ideas. Distinguish ideas with lots of directions to choose from. Look for patterns to figure out where your interest lies. You will feel more passionate about writing about something that genuinely interests you.

Narrow your list down to three possible topics. Taking your brainstorm list as a guide, cross out less interesting ideas until three potential topics or related keywords are left, which may just be narrower areas of focus you'd like to explore rather than cohesive thesis statements.

2) Performing research to select a broad topic. Dig deeper with the encyclopedia. Use encyclopedias to search for the key terms in the three potential topics. Read the searched papers, and jot down all interesting facts or important information you find, which will help you understand the topics at hand more thoroughly.

Read present newspaper articles about your broad topics. Search the databases of reputable newspapers for your topic keywords to find the current papers about your topics. In this way, you may see whether you should consider any new or crucial developments as you choose an area to write about. Save the URLs of any particularly good or helpful articles, because they may be useful sources for you later on. This information can also help you formulate a Works Cited list.

Consult a librarian. Make an appointment with a librarian at your school or public library. Bring any notes you've taken about your early study. Discuss your possible topics with the librarian and ask what unique books or databases might be relevant to your research. This may guide you to new perspectives on your potential topics.

Consult an expert. An expert in the field may have a deeper understanding of your topic ideas. They can provide you with in-depth and specific expertise or advice.

Be wary of using online sources. For scholarly articles, sites like Wikipedia are generally not permitted. Nevertheless, a site like Google Scholar can be used to find quality sources. Remember to choose sources that are factual, instead of opinionated, and that conform to any guidelines provided by your professor.

Determine which topics have the most sources to draw from. After your preliminary research, determine which potential topics have lots of critical resources and which have fewer, because you'll need lots of good materials to support your thesis later.

Choose a potential topic for your paper based on your research. The process of better understanding the topics may have helped you figure out which area is most interesting to you. Compare your interest with what you've found out and the resources available. An area of high interest with a lot of resources is ideal.

3) Refining your broader topic. Phrase your topic as a research question. Using your preliminary research as a guide, turn your broad idea into a research question that you will try to answer with your paper. It can be helpful to consider the relationship between your keywords. Did one make or influence the other? Did they happen or live concurrently?

Narrow the scope of your question by adding detail. Specify your question so you are uniquely discussing the topic. The best way to do this is to restrict the topic by adding conditions, like limitations about geography, time frame, or population.

Form a thesis statement. Now, use your preliminary research to provide a basic answer to the question you formulated. This will be the topic of your paper and the idea which you centralize deeper research around. The answer might be clear in your opinion according to what you've read, otherwise you should revisit some papers and sources since you've narrowed your topic.

2. Quick Ways to Choose a Good Topic for a Thesis

Before starting a research topic, the first thing is to consider where your passion lies, what subjects you master, and analyze your environment, and the time you must devote to research. A thesis should not only be seen as work associated with the subject but should also be a contribution to the subject in which a present issue is questioned, and different angles and ways of analyzing it that are important to the subject are indicated. Keep this in mind when selecting your theme, which is extremely effective on how to choose a thesis topic for a master's degree.

A good thesis topic must be a well-crafted topic, but you can't go around the bush. You should, from the beginning, define the topic that you will work well, and you can detail it in the introduction of the thesis to make readers know what it will be and how it will be addressed. You will not be able to study a subject without previous studies referring to the study variable. If the variable is complex, you can find data on the dimensions of the variable, additionally, you need plenty of materials and sources to be able to refer to in preparing your thesis and produce quality work with significant academic support; for this you can get help from the university repository.

Choosing a suitable thesis topic is a hard and key point to perform quality work. The following are some supportive tips to achieve it.

1) List possible topics. Before starting, it is recommended to list your preferential topics in a broader sense. If you are working in an institution, it is advisable to address a problem related to your workplace. Then you will have a first guide on the topics you would like to work on.

2) Check the background. A good alternative is to check the repositories of your university of study, in addition to the networks of scientific journals, which will offer you a broader horizon of the potential topics that you will study. Hard as it might be, it is an ideal tool to eliminate options or find ideas more enriching.

3) According to your strengths and abilities. You must have an interest in the chosen topic, therefore you do not get bored, you can maintain a positive attitude towards the proposal and you can be devoted to it for a while. Spend all the time necessary to select the topic. An interesting topic will also be a contribution to the subject and a differential for the thesis.

4) Define the subject. The secret of a good thesis topic is that it is well-defined. That is to say, it is simple but meanwhile allows you to dig deeply enough. It is perfect to pick a specific idea that you can expand as research requires. You must define, from the beginning, the topic you are going to work on; you may detail it in the introduction of the thesis so that readers know well what will be studied and how it will be addressed.

5) Available time. It prepares a specific schedule, allocates schedules for the completion of the thesis and establishes a period of the prior investigation. Managing work time well is the secret key to a well-done thesis.

6) It must represent a contribution to your career. A thesis is not only working on a topic related to the subject but must be a contribution to the career.

7) You should not limit your subsequent studies. Your thesis should help you advance your career and be conducive to further studies and insights. If, for instance, you study psychology and, in the future, you want to take treating children as your work, your thesis should be oriented to this field to ensure better preparation on the subject.

3.2 Literature Searching and Reviewing

3.2.1　What Is Literature Searching and Reviewing?

Literature searching is the act of searching databases and the Internet effectively to find key literature on your research topic. Literature reviewing is the reading and reviewing of a subject in the form of a written piece of work. Searching for literature is an important part of the research process—whether you are just beginning to scope out a project, or conducting a full literature review for your dissertation. Your search is part of your workflow. Study and research are iterative processes, which include searching for literature. This will be guided by your question or topic, which defines where and how you search. As you search and find items, you will interact with them critically and take notes. These ideas will help you refine your topic further and make decisions about what to do next.

Searching for existing literature will help you figure out:

- what other researchers have written about a specific topic;
- what is known and unknown—this is important when trying to identify gaps in research;
- how your work links to previous research;
- how your work is doing something new.

3.2.2　Literature Searching: Where and How

There are many resources for literature searching, and some typical resources for literature searching include the library, databases, search engines, and so forth.

1) The library. A classification system is used in most university libraries, called the Dewey Decimal Classification System, in which each subject will have its reference number. By the time you are doing literature searching, you should know very well the way that your institutional library works.

When you have located an area with books on your topic, look at the other books there. When you find a relevant text, look at the bibliography to find key authors. Once you have several books on the topic, you may find the same names again and again in the reference lists. Return to the catalog and try to find a book by the author who is being cited. Reading original work is better than quoting from secondary sources. Scan the books for keywords. Save the substantial amount of material in that book for reading later on.

Most libraries in universities provide online access to a large number of journals where you can search for articles and download them in PDF format for free. If you are unaware of a specialist journal, try searching the databases to identify what journals most frequently show up in your search.

2) Databases. Normally several databases are listed and accessed through your library web pages. You will have to register with them and then you can use any of these databases, which contain bibliographic records of literature. When you have logged on as a user and found records of interesting papers in the databases, you will see a link to the journal from which you can conveniently download a PDF of the paper.

Online resources change very often, so it is not feasible to go into detail about them in a textbook. If you have difficulty in using these resources, you had better consult a librarian or use the help field on that resource.

A citation is a reference to another person's work. Academics use citations to support an argument or to make a point. Citation indexes such as the Web of Knowledge involve the searcher looking for an author. Results will demonstrate other published papers that have referenced that author in a certain way, which is very useful when you have found a key text and wonder who else has cited that text and which often brings further references for your review.

3) Search engines. It may seem that the quickest way to begin your literature search is using a basic search engine, however, this method may lead to some pitfalls. Google, as a search engine, enjoys the greatest popularity and it can be very helpful. However, it can also yield hundreds, thousands or even millions of hits for one search term, which is certainly not a sensible start to your literature search.

Search engines like Google use "robots" or "spiders", which go out and search the text of web pages to construct the databases that you search. The "hits" at the top of the list are based on the engine's way of ranking pages, and it does not guarantee that those pages are good, reliable sources of information. Beware when searching on the Internet, you may encounter many bogus or unreliable sites that you must avoid in your academic work.

Except for the pitfalls, it is admitted that these large search engines can help you locate a source you have an interest in. Searching databases or search engines can become much easier when you understand how they function. Most search facilities use Boolean logic, which allows three types of basic search "AND", "OR" and "NOT".

4) Other resources. There might be other resources that are important for your topic, which generally fall into three categories:

- Official statistics. Official statistics can help provide basic evidence of the importance of your research as a sound start to the literature review. You may visit the web pages of the Government Department relevant to your research area, where official publications can often be found and downloaded.

- Charities or specialist organizations. Usually, key charities or organizations working in the area have a range of information and publications on their web pages. For a small fee, researchers can visit their libraries which contain rare books and articles.

- Other ad hoc resources. Sometimes you will find other web resources that do not fall into the above two areas, such as the site of a specific research group or the website of people interested in the topic. Pay attention to the quality of these resources.

3.3 Outlining, Drafting and Revising

3.3.1 Outlining

Outlining is a strategy for writing a paper, in which your paper can be broken into sections and subsections. An outline is a map of your essay, which manifests what information each part will contain, and in what order. An outline can be defined as an ordered list of the main writing points of an essay or another type of academic paper. An outline can help you better organize and define your subject matter, topic and subtopics so that you can write your paper in a logical progression from the initial thesis statement throughout the supporting paragraphs and finally to the conclusion.

Before writing an outline, you should have an argument, thesis, or hypothesis around which your outline will focus. This main idea may change over the process of writing; nevertheless, you ought to have something around which to build your outline as you proceed.

Before starting your outline, it is essential to:

- Define your purpose. What is the reason for choosing this particular topic? What do you hope to learn? What are you hoping to share with your audience?

- Determine who your audience is. Knowing whom exactly you are writing for will help you refine your paper.
- Develop your thesis statement. After you've read over the main content on the subject you were assigned, develop a working thesis. It is likely that you write multiple drafts before pinning down a thesis statement worth keeping.

To write your thesis statement, you should consider:

- Are there any gaps in the content available on the topic?
- Is there anything unresolved or controversial about the topic?
- Have any changes in analysis, methodology, or data occurred that may bring new evidence to a previously studied subject?
- Has there been any economic, social or other impact?
- What literature would anyone care to read on this topic?

After you have developed a far-reaching thesis statement, put it at the top of the outline heading.

Organize your outline in the format that fits into the structure required for the type of paper. You can employ the most suitable organizational patterns for you and your paper, once you understand your organizational tools.

When writing a lab report or an academic journal article, you may begin by setting a skeleton of the outline in IMRAD form. Then subsections can be added in each section to specify pieces of content to be written.

After building your outline, you may reorganize your ideas by arranging them in a different order. Moreover, while you are writing you may make some discoveries and can always adjust or deviate from the outline as needed. You may need to move things around, conduct more research, or cut off some points. Remember, an outline is merely an organizational tool and not fixed, while writing is a changing process. If you don't find outlining helpful, you can work on developing your writing practice.

It is advisable to create your outline before starting to write the paper because it will help organize the paper and also help you ensure that all of the elements are included.

3.3.2 Drafting

Drafting, in the writing process, is the stage where you start to write. It is sometimes regarded as the second step of the writing process, when you write the initial sentences that clearly express your concept or ideas. After you've outlined your thesis, you may get ready to structure it into your rough draft. In drafting you develop a complete first version of a piece of writing, but it is certainly not the final version. A first draft serves as a working version that you will later improve.

To begin your first draft, you may follow the guidelines and the suggestions below:

- Make the writing process work for you. Use any approaches to push forward the writing process.
- Keep in mind your writing purpose and the needs of your audience. Address those needs as much as possible.
- Be aware of including every key structural part of an essay: a thesis statement as a part of your introductory paragraph, three or more body paragraphs as described in your outline, and a concluding paragraph. Then add an appealing title to attract readers.
- Write paragraphs of a proper length for your writing assignment.
- Develop your paragraphs and your ideas according to your topic outline or your sentence outline. Each main idea is the topic of a new paragraph. Elaborate it with the supporting details and the sub-points of those details that you included in your outline.
- In general, write your introduction and conclusion last, after you have fleshed out the body paragraphs.

In your drafting, the following writing strategies may be helpful:

1) Start with free writing. In free writing, you follow the impulses of your mind, letting thoughts and ideas appear to you without advanced deliberation. This writing strategy encourages inspiration and helps brainstorm concepts to pin down what will be the core of your writing. This step helps you concentrate when you're drafting your body paragraphs.

2) Organize your information. In your drafting, find your thesis statement before starting your introductory paragraph. Solidifying your viewpoint gives you a way to figure out which pieces will go where. Structure your paragraphs logically and integrate all the necessary information (you can always revise later).

3) Elaborate on ideas. Flesh out the meat of your essay, supporting the topic sentences of each body paragraph with research-related information. Fill in any gaps left behind by your outline (if applicable).

4) Write a complete draft. Through drafting, you should try to get the entire first version of your piece down. The drafting process is designed to quickly put down and organize your ideas from start to finish so it shouldn't take too long, which benefits not only time but also the writing process, too. An ending will give you something to work towards, help you view the big picture of your piece, and know whether it is as strong as expected. The ending can also keep you focused and motivated (even if it's not the conclusion in your final draft).

5) Forgo the urge to proofread. Proofreading is one of the final writing steps. When you are drafting, ignore perfect spelling and sentence structure, and just organize and detail the information for your targeted audience—consider page or word count during the second or third drafts.

3.3.3 Revising

By undertaking revising, you can greatly improve your essay. Revising is among the important elements of the writing process because even experienced writers need to improve their drafts and rely on peers. When revising, you take a second look at your ideas. You try to make your ideas clearer, more accurate, more interesting, or more persuasive by adding, cutting, moving, or changing information.

The following strategies may help you get the best out of your revisions:

- Take a break. You take pride in what you wrote, but you may be too close to it to make changes. Stay away from your writing for a few hours or even a day till you can review it objectively.
- Ask your supervisors for feedback and constructive criticism.
- Ask yourself whether your readers will be satisfied or not and why.
- Use the resources available in your college, such as the writing lab. Try them over to look at your first drafts from a fresh perspective and keep using the useful ones.

Don't respond negatively to the words "critic", "critical", and "criticism". As a writer and a thinker, you should learn to be critical of yourself in a positive manner and build high expectations for your work. You should also develop your perception and trust your ability to fix what needs fixing. For this, you should learn where to look.

1. Creating Unity and Coherence

With unity in a piece of writing, all the ideas in each paragraph and the entire essay are organized in a sensible and logical order. With coherence, the ideas flow smoothly and the wording clearly shows how one idea leads to another within a paragraph and from paragraph to paragraph. You may find problems with unity and coherence by reading your writing aloud and listening for the clarity and flow of your ideas. Find places that confuse you, and take a note to yourself about how to fix them.

When you reread your writing for revisions, look for each type of problem separately. In other words, read it the first time to identify problems with unity, and read it a second time to locate problems with coherence. You may follow the same practice during many steps of the writing process. Transitions can help the writing flow smoothly, so they are often used to denote the relation of ideas in their sentences and paragraphs. Transitions cannot only improve coherence but give a mature feel to your essays.

Many writers make revisions on a printed copy and then transfer them to the version on-screen. They usually use a small arrow called a caret ($\wedge$) to show where to insert an addition or correction.

2. Being Clear and Concise

Some writers write a first draft methodically and painstakingly, while others unleash lots of words to get out everything they need to say. Do you prefer either of these writing styles? Or is your style somewhere in between? If you tend to write very much, you will have to cut unnecessary words. If you tend to be vague or imprecise in your wording, you will have to replace overly general words with specific expressions.

3. Identifying Wordiness

Remember too many words may not necessarily appeal more to the audience or better fit the purpose. By eliminating wordiness you can make your ideas clear, direct, and straightforward. Here are two common examples of wordiness to look for in your draft:

1) **Sentences with unneeded phrases.** Be judicious when you use phrases such as "in terms of", "with a mind to", "on the subject of", "as to whether... or not", "more or less", "as far as…is concerned", and other similar expressions. You can use a more direct way to state your point.

2) **Sentences in the passive voice or with forms of the verb "to be".** Sentences with passive-voice verbs often create confusion because the subject of the sentence does not act. Sentences are clearer when the subject of the sentence performs the action and is followed by a strong verb. Use strong active-voice verbs in place of forms of "to be". Avoid passive voice when you can.

4. Completing a Peer Review

After working so closely with a piece of writing, you often need objective feedback from readers who can respond only to the words on the page. When you are ready, you can show your drafts to someone you trust for an honest response about their strengths and weaknesses.

Then you can evaluate the feedback and assess what is most helpful to revise your draft. This process is called peer review. You can pair with a classmate and find specific ways to improve each other's essays. Although you may not be comfortable sharing your writing at first, keep in mind that every writer is striving for the same goal: a final draft that caters to the audience and the purpose. Keeping a positive attitude when offering.

5. Using Feedback Objectively

Peer feedback is designed to collect constructive criticism of your essay. Your peer reviewer is your first real audience, and you can know what perplexes and satisfies a reader so that you can strengthen your work before sharing the final draft with more readers (or your targeted audience).

You do not have to incorporate all recommendations your peer reviewer makes. However, if you notice a pattern in the responses you receive from peer reviewers, you should heed that feedback in future writing. For instance, if you receive consistent comments about a need for more research, then you may need to conduct more research in future assignments.

You might receive feedback from more than one reader as you share different stages of your revised draft. In this case, some feedback may be made by readers who do not understand the assignment or who are less involved with and enthusiastic about it. You should evaluate the responses you get according to two important standards:

- Whether the feedback supports the purpose of the assignment;
- Whether the suggested revisions are proper for the audience.

Then, accept or reject revision feedback using these criteria.

3.4 Proofreading and Publishing

3.4.1 Proofreading

Written communication is used almost everywhere in our daily lives. It's important to reread the text to make sure it's written accurately and clearly. That is why we need proofreading. Learning how to proofread your work for writing errors can help you avoid confusion and miscommunication. Proofreading is to carefully check for mistakes in a text before it is published or shared.

The word "proofreading" originated from the traditional publishing industry. Before digital publishing got popular, publishers would print an early copy of a text (the "proof"). A final review of the proof was conducted by a proofreader to find any grammatical, spelling, and formatting mistakes or inconsistencies. Although the manuscript or text might have gone through top editing, line editing, and copy editing, certain mistakes can still slip past those review stages. Proofreading, though, is the last chance to fix any mistakes that might have been missed before publication. In the publishing industry, proofreaders conventionally read through a printed "proof copy" of the text and mark corrections using specialized proofreading marks. In other areas, however, professional proofreaders usually deal with digital texts and make corrections directly using the track changes feature in Microsoft Word Docs.

The following strategies can help you improve your proofreading skills and find errors before your paper is submitted.

1) Edit your writing first. Before you start proofreading, ensure you have completely revised and edited your work, because it is pointless spending time correcting minor mistakes if the whole sections or paragraphs might be removed or rewritten later. Begin proofreading once a final draft is ready.

2) Take a break from the text. Set your work aside. When you have been working on the same text for a long time, it gets more difficult to notice errors. Before proofreading, step away from your work for a while so that you can review it with fresh eyes. You should wait at least one or two days before final proofreading, however, even a half-hour break makes a difference if you have a deadline to meet.

3) **Proofread a printout.** Reading your words on a printed page is another helpful strategy for spotting things that might have been missed on the screen. If the final version will be printed, this is also a good opportunity to ensure correct and consistent formatting on the page.

4) **Use digital shortcuts.** While reading from print can help you notice mistakes, word-processing software can help you correct them efficiently. You may run a spell check—but do not depend on the computer to spot all errors. If you've frequently misspelled a specific word, inconsistently capitalized a term, or switched between U.K. and U.S. English, you may use the Find and Replace function to correct the same error throughout the text. Be careful, and do not use "replace all". Check every replacement to avoid making more mistakes!

5) **Learn from your mistakes.** Heed the recurring mistakes in the document, which can help you avoid them in the future. Knowing what to look out for is the hardest part of proofreading. It is easier to spot obvious typos, but subtle errors in grammar and punctuation might be more difficult to notice.

3.4.2 Publishing

Publishing is the final stage of the writing process. This is the presentation or appearance of your work. For publishing, you need to know that there are many types of publications, i.e. books, journal articles, conference proceedings. etc. Different types of publications obey their own formats, features and styles, which have critical influence on your writing content and your writing process. You may refer to the late chapter for details.

📖 Review Questions

1. What is a research topic? What is a research question? What is a research title?

2. What are literature searching and reviewing? What are the sources for literature searching?

3. What are outlining, drafting and revising respectively? What are the strategies for drafting? What are the steps and techniques for revising?

4. What is proofreading?

4
Chapter

Typical Components of Scientific Writing

Learning Objectives

After reading this chapter, you should be able to:

1. Understand the typical structure of an Introduction;
2. Know the reasons for and the ways of conducting a literature review;
3. Know how to write the Methodology section for research articles, theses and dissertations;
4. Know the structure and style of a Discussion section in scientific writing.

Chapter Lead-in: Typically, scientific research papers contain all or most of the following sections: Title, By-line and Affiliation, Abstract, Introduction, Literature Review, Method, Results, Discussion, Conclusion, Summary, Acknowledgments and References. This chapter introduces the writing of the Introduction, the Literature Review, the Methodology, the Discussion as well as the Title, the Abstract, and the Conclusion sections respectively.

4.1 Writing the Introduction

4.1.1 Introduction in Scientific Writing: What and Why

The Introduction constitutes the first section of a scholarly article. It is mainly designed to disseminate basic information to the readers without obligating them to investigate previous publications and to provide clues as to the results of the present study. For this purpose, the subject of the article should be completely reviewed, and the aim of the study should be presented immediately after discussing the basic references. Introduction sections of academic articles are like the gates of a city. It is a presentation aiming at introducing itself to the readers, and capturing their attention. Attractiveness, clarity, piquancy, and analytical capacity of the presentation will attract the readers to read the following sections of the article.

It is useful to analyze the content of the Introduction section under three headings. Firstly, you should provide information about the general topic of the article in light of the current literature which leads to disclosing the objective of the article. You should make a clear, and precise explanation of the topic in the light of the current literature as if the audience knows little of the subject. Do not plunge into the problem or the solution frantically, because you may push the reader into the dilemma of either screening the literature about the subject matter or refraining from reading the article. You should present updated, and robust information in the Introduction section.

Then you should address the specific subject matter, bring forth the problem, and discuss fundamental references related to the topic. At this point, you should try to reduce the problems to one issue. There might be more than one problem, however, this new issue and its solution should be the subject matter of another article. And remember to express problems clearly.

Finally, you should describe recommendations for solutions, in other words, you should communicate the aim. In that order, the reader can track the problem, and its solution from his or her perspective in light of the current literature. Otherwise, inadequate information, inability to clarify the problem, and sometimes concealing the solution will keep the reader who wants to get new information away from reading the article.

In addition to the above-mentioned information about the Introduction section, you may also consider the following points:

- Abbreviations should be given following their explanations in the Introduction section (their explanations in the summary do not count);
- Simple present tense should be used;
- References should be selected from updated publications with a higher impact factor, and prestigious sourcebooks;
- Avoid mysterious and confusing expressions, and construct clear sentences aimed at problematic issues and their solutions;
- The sentences should be attractive, tempting and comprehensible.

Writing a good Introduction is very important, for you never get a second chance to make a first impression. The Introduction of your paper will leave your readers with the first impression of your argument, your writing style, and the general quality of your work. A vague, disorganized, error-filled, off-the-wall, or boring introduction will create a negative impression. On the contrary, a concise, engaging, and well-written introduction will make your readers think highly of you, your analytical skills, your writing, and your article.

Your Introduction, as an important road map for the remainder of your paper, conveys a lot of information to your readers. You can let them know what your topic is, why it is important, and how you plan to proceed with your discussion. In many scientific disciplines, your introduction should contain a thesis that will assert your main argument. Your introduction should also help the reader understand the kinds of information you will use to make that argument and the general organization of the paragraphs and pages that will follow.

Hopefully, the Introduction will draw your readers' interest, making them want to read the remainder of your paper.

4.1.2　Introduction Writing: Steps and Strategies

1. Steps to Write an Introduction

In the Introduction section of a research paper, you put forward your topic and approach for the reader. There are a few key goals:

- Present your topic and interest the reader;
- Provide background or generalize current research;
- Position your method;
- Specify your research problem;

- Outline the paper's organization.

The Introduction may slightly differ to suit different papers. For example, papers presenting the results of original empirical research may require a different Introduction from the ones constructing an argument involving various sources. For either kind of research paper, you may follow these five steps to come up with an effective introduction.

Step 1: Introduce your topic. The introduction is designed to first inform the reader of your topic and explain why it's interesting or important. You may strengthen it with a strong opening hook, which is a striking opening sentence that points out the relevance of your topic. An interesting fact or statistic, a strong statement, a provoking question, or a concise anecdote will do. Your hook need not be exceptionally impressive or creative. You should not pursue catchiness while neglecting clarity and relevance. Remember the key is to take the reader to your topic and present your ideas.

Step 2: Describe the background. This section of the introduction is subject to the approach your paper is taking. In a more persuasive paper, some general background is laid out here. After you have attracted your reader's attention, narrow down a bit more, providing background and specifying your topic. Provide only the most related background information, because the introduction isn't the place to get too in-depth; if more background is needed for your paper, you can get to it in the body. In a more empirical paper, this part reviews previous research and illustrates how yours fits in. If your paper describes original research, you should provide an overview of the latest research that has already been done. This is a miniature literature review—a sketch of the existing state of research into your topic, summarized in a few sentences. Your search is not necessarily as extensive as that in a full literature review, but a clear sense of the relevant research is crucial to inform your work. Start with the research that has been conducted, and end with limitations or gaps in the research that you plan to address.

Step 3: Establish your research problem. The next step is to explain how your research fits in and what problem it responds to. In an argumentative research paper, you can make a simple statement about the problem you will analyze, and what is original or significant about your argument. In an empirical research paper, try to guide the problem based on your discussion of the literature. Consider the following questions:

- What research gap is your work going to fill?
- What limitations in the past work does it respond to?
- What contribution to knowledge does it make?

Step 4: Specify your objective(s). Now you'll get into the specifics of what you plan to discover or convey in your paper. You can frame this in various ways. An argumentative paper presents a thesis statement, while an empirical paper usually raises a research question (sometimes with a hypothesis as to the answer). In argumentative papers, the thesis statement establishes the position for which the remainder of the paper will provide evidence and arguments. You can present it clearly and directly in one or two sentences, without writing specific arguments for it at this point. In empirical papers, the research question is the question for you to respond to. You may present your research question clearly and directly, with a minimum of discussion at this point. In the remainder of the paper, you will discuss and investigate this question, and you just need to point it out here. You can frame your research question either directly or indirectly. If hypotheses are tested in your research, you should present them with your research question. You should state them in the past tense, as the hypothesis will have been tested by the time you are composing your article.

Step 5: Map out your paper. As the final part of the introduction, you may write a concise overview of the remainder of the paper. If your paper is structured according to the standard scientific format, i.e., IMRAD, you do not necessarily have to compose it. But if your paper is structured rather differently, you are obliged to map it out for the reader. If included, the overview should be brief, direct, and written in the present tense.

2. Strategies for Writing an Effective Introduction

Begin by considering the question (or questions) you are trying to address. Your entire essay will deal with this question with your introduction as the first step toward that end. Your thesis will be the direct answer to the question, and your thesis will probably be included in your introduction, so you can use the question as a jumping-off point.

Make sure how general or broad your opening will be. Remember that even a "big picture" opening needs to be around your topic. When writing, you must place your ideas in context which doesn't have to be as big as the whole universe.

Try writing your introduction last. You do not necessarily have to write your introduction first, which is not always the most effective way to write a good introduction because at the beginning of the writing process, you likely do not know exactly what you are going to argue. Sometimes you even set out thinking that you want to argue a specific point but end up arguing something slightly or even greatly different by the time you have almost completed the paper. Through the writing process, you constantly organize your ideas, ponder over complex matters, refine your thoughts, and craft a complicated argument. Therefore, an introduction written at the beginning of that discovery process may not necessarily represent what you have at the end. Sometimes it's easiest to just write up all of your evidence first and then write the introduction last, in which way you can guarantee that your introduction will cover the body of your paper.

If you need to write some sort of introduction to start the writing process, you may write a tentative introduction first and then change it later. Just remember to return to it later and rewrite it if needed.

Start your introduction with something appealing to the readers. The following options (noticing that they may suit all types of papers) may help:

- an intriguing example;
- a provocative quotation closely related to your argument;
- a puzzling scenario;
- a thought-provoking question;
- a vivid and maybe unexpected anecdote.

Be careful with your first sentence, making sure that it says something useful in an engaging and polished way.

4.2 Writing the Literature Review

4.2.1 Literature Review in Scientific Writing: What and Why

1. What Is Scientific Literature?

In the *Cambridge Dictionary*, literature is defined as all the information relating to a subject, especially information written by experts. Scientific literature is the major medium for disseminating the findings of scientific research and permanently recording the collective achievements of the scientific circle over time. This scientific knowledge base is made up of the individual "end products" of scientific research results and continuously grows as new research is done based on earlier research. This new research may contribute to, substantiate, modify, refine or refute current knowledge on a particular topic.

Typically, there are three kinds of scientific literature: primary literature, secondary literature and tertiary literature. Primary literature refers to publications that report the results of original scientific research, based on direct observation, use of statistical records, interviews, or experimental methods, of actual practices or the actual impact of practices or policies. Primary literature involves measuring, evaluating, and testing hypotheses, so sometimes it is also called empirical research. Primary literature must provide sufficient information to enable another researcher (with the proper skills) to experiment again. It is written by researchers and is usually published in a peer-reviewed journal. Primary literature may also include conference papers, technical reports, theses, and dissertations.

Secondary literature refers to publications that interpret, evaluate and compress what is known on specific topics. This kind of literature sometimes synthesizes information from primary sources to arrive at new conclusions or rewrites it in a new form. Generally, secondary literature presents some new information or criticism on the topics discussed. Secondary literature may consist of review articles (such as meta-analysis and systematic reviews), monographs, encyclopedias, textbooks, treatises, handbooks and manuals.

Tertiary literature is designed to offer an overview of key research results and an introduction to principles and practices within the discipline. It is primarily used as a finding aid for primary and secondary literature and does not usually present any new information.

Primary literature is the most important type to search for the latest information on a research area. Secondary literature and tertiary literature are there to assist the reader in finding and comprehending the primary literature, but they are the first-hand accounts of actual research which help the reader know what has been done, and what discoveries researchers have made.

2. What Is Literature Review?

A literature review refers to an all-directional overview of previous research concerning a particular topic. Sometimes it is an independent investigation of how an idea or field of inquiry has grown over time. Nevertheless, in most cases, it's part of a scientific paper, thesis or dissertation setting out the context against which a study is conducted.

A literature review tells the reader both what is known about a topic and what is not known yet, thereby setting up the principle or need for a new investigation. That is what the actual study which the review is attached to intends to do. As an overview, a successful literature review consists of all of the main themes and sub-themes found within the general topic of the study. These themes and sub-themes are usually integrated with the approaches or discoveries of the previous research. Also, a literature review makes preparations for the purpose and methods of the original research being reported in a paper.

Articles found in academic journals and books comprise the most common and most appropriate sources for a literature review. Whereas, the articles on certain research topics may not be accessible. Then you may turn to other commonly accepted resources, such as governmental publications and newspaper articles, etc. A literature review should locate and discuss/explain all of the major points or discoveries of a particular topic, including both classic (if available) and the most recent studies to show a deep understanding of the topic chosen.

3. Why to Conduct a Literature Review

In an academic paper writing, the literature review is often seen as a formality. It is misunderstood as simply a list of all sorts of studies about the topic and nothing more. The literature review is very important to a successful experimental report or research paper for several reasons.

Primarily, literature reviews force you to access as much information as possible related to the topic at hand. This will be not only beneficial for the learning process but also helpful for the writing. Second, literature reviews convince readers that you have a solid knowledge of the topic, which brings credibility to you and integrity to the paper's comprehensive argument. Meanwhile, by studying all previous literature, you may find the weaknesses and shortcomings of prior literature. This will not only help in arguing for the need for a specific research question to explore but also assist in better forming the argument for why further research is needed. Thereby the literature review of a research report foreshadows your study.

Remember that readers cannot be familiar with all of the pertinent background and preexisting knowledge about any topic, because scientific knowledge (about all topics) increases rapidly, and it is a challenge to keep up on any topic. In light of the cumulative nature of science, reliable accounts of prior research form a necessary condition for orderly knowledge building.

4.2.2 Classification of Literature Reviews

Different kinds of literature reviews can be classified according to the characteristics of focus, goal, perspective, coverage, organization, and audience.

1. The "Focus" Classification

The first characteristic is the focus of the review, including four potential foci: research outcomes, research methods, theories or practices or applications.

Maybe literature reviews concentrating on research outcomes are the most common. An outcomes-oriented review may help identify a paucity of information on a specific research outcome, thus justifying the need for outcome research.

Methodological reviews focusing on research methods instead of research outcomes have been used in various areas to advance research practice. In a methodological review, research methods in the chosen area are studied to find important variables, measures, and methods of analysis and inform outcomes-oriented studies. The methodological review also assists in finding methodological strengths and weaknesses in a body of research and examines how research practices vary across groups, times, or settings. If the prior research has been methodologically inappropriate, a methodological review may also yield sound principles that can justify your research.

A review of theories can help know what theories already exist, the relationships between them, and to what degree the present theories have been studied. For instance, if the paper intends to develop a new theory, a theoretical review is the right option. Concerning the basic research principles, a theoretical review can help point out that the existing theories are inadequate, and justify that a new theory should be put forward.

Finally, literature reviews can be concentrated on practices or applications. For instance, a review might focus on how an intervention has been carried out or how some people plan to apply some practice. Concerning a research rationale, this fourth kind of review can help establish a practical need not presently being met.

2. The "Goal" Classification

The goal of many reviews is to generalize and integrate discoveries across units, treatments, outcomes, and settings; to solve a debate within a field; or to bridge the language used across fields. For instance, meta-analysis is a common review technique in which the basic goal is to synthesize quantitative results across studies. In other reviews, the goal might be to critically analyze prior studies, find central issues or explain a line of argument within an area.

A dissertation review usually has multiple goals. If it is solely a review, it might lay emphasis on integration, but it also may critically analyze the research, identify central issues, or explicate an argument. Nevertheless, if the author intends to justify later research with the literature review, the goal will emphasize critical analysis of the literature to find a weakness and propose to modify it with dissertation research. Either way, the author must integrate reviews to offer the reader the big picture.

3. The "Perspective" Classification

In qualitative primary research, review authors usually uncover their preoccupied prejudices and talk about how those biases might have affected the review. Or, usually in quantitative primary research, authors may claim a neutral perspective and present the review results as facts. The perspective relies largely on whether the review is carried out in the quantitative or qualitative traditions. Because secondary research (i.e., review research) methods parallel primary research methods, it is likely that the author of a qualitative review sticks to the qualitative tradition and uncovers prejudices and the author of a quantitative review sticks to the quantitative tradition and takes a neutral position. This decision will be subject to the specific case.

4. The "Coverage" Classification

When carrying out a review, it is a crucial step to decide how wide to cast the net. There are four coverage scenarios. An exhaustive review is designed to find and review all available pieces of research on a chosen topic, published or unpublished. Nevertheless, it may take more time than is available to locate every piece of study. The key is to specify the population to manage the number of articles to review, which is referred to as an exhaustive review with selective citations. For instance, the reviewer may only go through articles published in journals, but not conference papers; of course, it is advisable to have a theoretical justification for the exclusion.

A third coverage method is to analyze a representative sample of articles and infer about all articles from that sample. Whereas, random sampling is by no means unfailing. Maybe a more reliable method is to pool evidence to prove that the representative sample is representative. The safest way may be to do both.

The fourth article selection approach is to take a purposive sample in which the reviewer analyzes merely the pivotal or central articles in an area. The key here is to persuade the reader that the chosen articles are the pivotal or central ones in an area, and just as importantly that the articles not chosen are not pivotal or central.

5. The "Organization" Classification

A review can be organized in many formats, among which the historical format, the conceptual format, and the methodological format are the most common ones. The review is written chronologically in the historical format, which is recommended when the emphasis is on the progression of research methods or theories, or on a change in practices over time.

A second common organizational strategy is established around concepts. For instance, the review may be centered around the propositions in a research rationale or, in a theoretically-focused review, organized according to the different theories in the literature. Finally, the literature review can be written methodologically, as in an empirical paper (i.e., introduction, method, results, and discussion). Sometimes it may be most effective to combine and/or match these organizational formats. For instance, the reviewer might begin with an introduction, define the method, and report the findings in a historical or conceptual format, then proceed to the discussion of findings, which is commonly used in meta-analytic reports.

6. The "Audience" Classification

The last characteristic is the audience. The supervisor and reviewers are the primary audiences for a dissertation; the scholars within the related area are the secondary audience. Do not write the literature review for a general, non-academic audience. What makes a good book is probably not what makes a good dissertation, and vice versa.

4.2.3　Literature Review Writing: Process and Techniques

1. The General Process of Literature Review

Conducting a literature review may involve the following steps: problem formulation, literature collection, literature evaluation, analysis and interpretation.

1) Problem formulation. After the proper kind of review has been decided, the focus falls on problem formulation. At this point you figure out what questions the literature review will address and identify clear standards to determine the inclusion, or exclusion, of an article in the review. In this step, it is crucial to distinguish literature review questions (i.e., questions that can be answered by reviewing the secondary research) from empirical research questions (i.e., questions that can be answered only through the primary research). The literature review is the main source of the empirical research question.

2) Literature collection. The literature (data) collection stage is designed to gather an exhaustive, semi-exhaustive, representative, or pivotal set of related articles. You should document the literature collection procedure with such detail that if other reviewers stick to the same procedures under the same conditions, they will find the same set of articles. The literature collection process usually starts with an electronic search of academic databases and the Internet. When conducting these searches, you must keep accurate and careful records of the date of each search, the databases searched, the keywords and keyword combinations used, and the number of records from each search.

Approximately only 10% of the articles for an exhaustive review come up in electronic searches. Then how to find the other 90%? The most effective approach is to search the references of the articles that have been located, identify the valid ones and find them, study their references, and repeat the process until no new pertinent articles turn up. When you have completed electronic and reference searching, you may ask experts in the area to check the list of references to see if any articles are missing. You should find a way to further prune the gathered articles. For instance, you can read the abstract or the title of each electronic record to identify the irrelevant studies and discard them. It is advisable to precisely record the process undertaken. After that, you can proceed to consider which of the remaining articles will be used in the literature review.

3) Literature evaluation. The literature (data) evaluation stage is designed to extract and evaluate the information from the articles that satisfied the standards for inclusion. First, you, according to the focus and goal of the review, devise a system for extracting data from the articles. For instance, if the focus is research outcomes and the goal is integration, you will extract research results data from every article and consider how to integrate those results. When you evaluate the data, it is advised to record the kinds of data extracted and the procedure used. Because it demands great detail, separate coding forms and a coding book might be used in this recording. The detail should guarantee that a second person could make more or less identical findings by following the documented procedure.

It is vital to carefully study the kinds of data to be extracted from every article and to thoroughly pilot test the coding book. Other kinds of data that should be extracted may be uncovered in the extraction process, which may make revision of the coding book necessary. Literature reviews usually analyze data about the quality of research. Whereas, there are controversies about the inclusion of low-quality articles in a review. Some suggest including only high-quality articles in a study, while others suggest including both high-quality and low-quality studies and presenting the differences between them. A goal of many reviews is to synthesize or integrate research results. Therefore, a universal metric or measure should be established into which all of the research results can be translated.

4) Literature analysis and interpretation. At the literature (data) analysis and interpretation stage, you are to make sense of the extracted data. If the goal of the literature review is integration, you now synthesize the data. According to the kind of data extracted, you will perform a quantitative, qualitative, or mixed-methods synthesis.

2. The Outlining Technique for Literature Review

In writing a successful literature review, outlining may be the most significant step, because a well-thought outline can be of much help in collecting important information and sources, saving time while writing, and contributing to a more clarified and powerful argument for readers.

At the word "outline", lots of people get worried, because they have not mapped out every point and sub-point. Those strict structures are not necessary. The outline just sketches what you plan to discuss, and how. Outlining serves three purposes; it functions as a mechanism for integrating and transforming ideas, a mechanism for sequencing those ideas, and a general plan for the composition.

First, you need to choose a general topic to study. Do not pick a narrow topic at the beginning, because it might severely limit the amount and quality of sources to be found. It is advisable to choose something of interest but not too specific of a focus. It is also crucial to remember that the topic can be modified or revised later on, which forms a natural progression of developing an outline. Throughout the outlining process, you may come across new ideas and research questions, which may broaden the scope of your argument and improve your on-going study.

The second process in outlining is providing evidence for the general topic and bringing it to a more specific focus. It is also a natural progression, which can be compared to building a puzzle. Every source for the general topic will probably bring out other applicable sources with their topics or subtopics. All of these are like puzzle pieces, which help complete the entire picture. From these sources, you may also identify all of the subtopics for the related topic, which can help you establish the criteria for dictating where and how to look for other useful sources. In this way, you will probably develop new ideas and fill some gaps before starting to write. Therefore, the notion of the outline is seen as being a "living" or "fluid" document. After you have crafted an initial draft, it is not merely acceptable but also expected to constantly alter the outline.

Furthermore, if an outline remains the same throughout the writing process, it probably will be an unsuccessful literature review because new ideas and areas of knowledge emerging during the process are not promptly pursued and included. Remember to accept the "living" nature of the outline, for every small change contributes to a more powerful and complete literature review. In a similar way, when you later work with your outline and write sentences, paragraphs, and sections, revision and alteration should be embraced. Here, the overall writing can be reckoned as the process of writing to understand and writing to be understood. The first goal is creating your outline and initial drafting of your manuscript. Once you write things down in a way that you can understand, your goal shifts (in your revised and final drafts of a manuscript) to writing for a reader to understand.

3. The Ending Technique for Literature Review

The end of the literature review, as the bridge to the current study, must clearly and concisely summarize what was present in the literature review without digging into the extensive and specific details. It should strike a delicate balance between the primary findings and the methodology of previous studies and explicate the need for the continued study of a certain research topic or maybe a new methodology.

Up to this point, the argument of the present study has been presented in providing the weaknesses or gaps in discoveries or the strengths/shortcomings of the methodology of previous research. At this point, nevertheless, the weaknesses in discoveries or the methodology of previous research are clearly stated. It is like a criminal prosecutor spending days telling a jury that an individual is guilty of a crime. The prosecutors may have had a few days to convince the jury of the individual's guilt (and do so by introducing then discussing/detailing individual pieces of evidence), but then at the end (in the closing argument) they have to summarize their argument and necessitate a particular result (like a guilty verdict) within a short time to persuade jurors. Readers can be compared to the jurors here. After reading the literature review, they need to understand what the topic is, all of the relevant literature on the topic, any weaknesses in previous discoveries/methodology, and what contribution this study will make to the further knowledge of this topic.

Following the above steps and making enough practice, you will naturally get the hang of writing a literature review. Of course, different topics may pose unique challenges; nevertheless, you will learn to identify the focus of the current topic, and know the kinds of necessary information to include, if you stick to the steps, processes, and organization discussed above. Additionally, learning how to write a good literature review will be of great help in synthesizing large amounts of information, recognizing arguments being made in readings across all disciplines, and understanding the structure of others' writings that may have been less apparent beforehand. A substantive and thorough literature review paves the way for doing substantive and thorough research. Therefore, learning how to write a good literature review matters for both the writing process and the learning process.

4.3 Writing the Methodology

4.3.1 Methodology in Scientific Writing: What and How

A research methodology is special techniques and various procedures implemented to define, choose, process, and make an analysis of data about a subject you've chosen. The Methodology section in your research paper helps people evaluate a paper's reliability and genuineness. The Research Methodology section of any academic research paper allows you to convince your readers that your research is useful and will contribute to your field of study. An effective research methodology is grounded in your overall approach—whether qualitative or quantitative—and adequately describes the methods you used. Justify why you chose those methods over others, then explain how those methods will provide answers to your research questions. It's quite important to spend enough time to create a successful research methodology for your paper.

As different kinds of methodologies, qualitative, quantitative and mixed methods can be over-simply distinguished by whether they focus on words, numbers or both, to make it easier to understand. Qualitative research focuses on collecting and analyzing words (written or spoken) and textual data, while quantitative research, on measurement and testing using numerical data. Qualitative analysis can also focus on other "softer" data points, like body language or visual elements. In research with exploratory objectives, it is common to use a qualitative methodology. For instance, a qualitative methodology can be applied to analyze people's perceptions about an event that happened. In contrast, a quantitative methodology is typically used in the research with confirmatory aims. For instance, a quantitative methodology may be applied to analyze the relationship between two variables or to test hypotheses. The mixed-methods methodology combines the best of both qualitative and quantitative methodologies to gain an integrated perspective and create a rich picture.

In a dissertation, thesis, or academic journal article (or almost any formal piece of research), you'll find a Research Methodology section which includes such aspects as:

- what data to collect (and what data to overlook);
- who to collect it from (in research, this is called "sampling design");
- how to collect it (this is called "data collection methods");
- how to analyze it (this is called "data analysis methods").

Sampling design is about deciding who you will collect your data from (i.e., your sample). Among many sample options, the two major kinds of sampling design are probability sampling and non-probability sampling. Probability sampling involves using a completely random sample from the group of people you're interested in (this group is called the "population"). By using a completely random sample, the results of your study can represent the entire group. That is to say, you can expect the same results across the entire population, without having to collect data from the entire group (which is often not possible for large groups). In contrast, non-probability sampling does not use a random sample. For instance, it might use a convenience sample, which means you only interview or survey accessible people (maybe your friends, family or colleagues), instead of a completely random sample (which may be hard to access owing to resource constraints). Typically the results from non-probability sampling are not generalizable.

How to collect data for your study? There are many different options, which can be categorized into the groups below:

- interviews (which can be unstructured, semi-structured or structured);
- focus groups and group interviews (which can bring together a small group of people to answer questions in a moderated setting);
- surveys (online or physical surveys);
- observations;
- documents and records;
- case studies.

The type of data collection method to use is determined by your comprehensive research aims and objectives, as well as practicalities and resource constraints. For instance, if you conduct exploratory research, you may go with qualitative methods like interviews and focus groups. On the contrary, if your research is designed to measure specific variables or test hypotheses, you should employ large-scale surveys that produce large volumes of numerical data.

Data analysis methods can be grouped according to whether the research is qualitative or quantitative. Popular data analysis methods in qualitative research include:

- qualitative content analysis;
- thematic analysis;
- discourse analysis;
- narrative analysis;
- grounded theory;
- interpretative phenomenological analysis (IPA).

Qualitative data analysis all begins with data coding, after which one (or more) analysis technique is applied.

4.3.2 Methodology Writing for Theses and Dissertations

In the Methodology section of your thesis or dissertation, you emphasize the philosophical foundations of your research and briefly present your specific research design choices. This section is designed to inform the reader about exactly how you designed your research and how you justified your design choices. The Methodology section should comprehensively report and explicate all the research design choices you made. For instance, the kind of research you conducted (e.g., qualitative or quantitative), how you collected your data, how you analyzed your data and who or where you collected data from (sampling).

When writing your Methodology section, you may notice that the exact structure and contents of the Methodology section will differ according to the area of research (e.g., humanities vs. chemistry vs. engineering) and the university. Thus, it's advisable to read the guidelines provided by your institution for clarity and, if possible, consult previous dissertations and theses from your university. Here we will talk about a typical structure for a Methodology section commonly found in the sciences, particularly the social sciences (e.g., psychology).

Before starting to write, you should draft a rough outline to have a clear direction. Don't just begin writing without knowing what will go where. Start with the end in mind.

1) Introduction. The Methodology section should have a concise introduction. In this part, you should restate the focus of your study, particularly the research aims. Your research design must be in line with your research aims, objectives and research questions, so it's necessary to remind the reader (and yourself!) where you intend to arrive with your design and methodology. In this part, You can also concisely discuss how you'll structure the section, which will help the reader know what to expect.

2) The research design. In the next part of your Methodology section, you should demonstrate your research design to the reader. In this part, you need to detail and justify all the important design choices in a logical, intuitive manner, which is the core of your Methodology section, so you should get specific. The following are the most common design choices you'll have to cover in the Methodology section.

Research philosophy. Research philosophy is the underlying beliefs (i.e., worldview) concerning how data about a phenomenon should be gathered, analyzed and used. Your research philosophy will act as the heart of your study and support all of the other research design choices, so you must know which philosophy you'll take and why you make that choice.

Research type. The research type is the next thing you will usually cover in your Methodology section. You may start by clarifying whether your research is inductive or deductive. With inductive research, the theory is developed from the ground up (i.e., from the collected data), and thus these studies are probably exploratory in approach. On the other hand, deductive research builds onto established theory with collected data, and hence these studies are likely to be confirmatory in terms of approach. You'll need to clarify whether your study takes a qualitative, quantitative or mixed-methods methodology. Due to a strong connection between this choice and your research philosophy, remember that your choices are strictly consistent. Again, when you compose this part, do not forget to explicitly justify your choices, for they build the foundation of your study.

Research strategy. Next, you'll need to present your research strategy (i.e., your research "action plan"). This research design choice refers to how you carry out your research based on the aims of your study. There are quite a few research strategies, such as experiments, case studies, ethnography, grounded theory, action research, and phenomenology. The right research strategy will rely on your research aims and research questions—in other words, what you're trying to find. Therefore, as with every other design choice, it's important to justify why you chose the research strategy as you did.

Time horizon. The next thing you should indicate in your Methodology section is the time horizon. There are two options: cross-sectional and longitudinal, meaning whether the data for your study were all collected at one point in time (i.e., cross-sectional) or at multiple points (i.e., longitudinal). Your choice here relies again on your research aims, objectives and research questions. Another important factor is the practical constraints—in other words, whether you have enough time for a longitudinal approach (which may involve collecting data over multiple years). Very often, you have to adopt a cross-sectional time horizon due to the time pressure of your program.

Sampling strategy. Next, you'll need to cover your chosen sampling strategy. There are two key categories of sampling, probability and non-probability sampling. Probability sampling refers to a random (and therefore representative) selection of participants from a population, while non-probability sampling involves selecting participants in a non-randomized (and therefore non-representative) way. For instance, selecting participants based on ease of access (this is called a convenience sample). The suitable sampling approach relies largely on what you're trying to develop in your study. Here practicalities and resource constraints also have an impact, for it can be difficult to access a truly random sample.

Design data collection method. Next up, you need to demonstrate how exactly you will collect the necessary data for your research. Your data collection method (or methods) will rely on the kind of data that you intend to collect—in other words, qualitative or quantitative data. As you may see, there is a tight connection between this part and the design choices you mapped out in earlier parts. It is vital to maintain a strong alignment between these sections.

Data analysis methods/techniques. The last key design choice that you need to cover is that of analysis techniques—in other words, after you've collected your data, how will you analyze it? Here it's crucial to be specific about your analysis methods and/or techniques, leaving no room for interpretation. Also, as with all choices in this section, you should justify every choice you make. What exactly you discuss here will rely largely on the kind of study you're undertaking (i.e., qualitative, quantitative, or mixed-methods). In this part, remember to demonstrate how you prepared your data for analysis, and what software you used (if any). For instance, quantitative data will often require some initial preparation like removing duplicates or incomplete responses. As always, do not forget to explicate both what you did and why you did it.

3) The methodological limitations. After you outline and justify the main research design choices, you may proceed to talk about the limitations of your design. Due to the constraints, you have to compromise between the perfect design and the practical and feasible design; therefore, your research design or methodology is usually imperfect. So you can discuss the compromise you have made in this part of your Methodology section. And remember to justify why you go with this design. You may encounter various methodological limitations in different studies, including common issues like time and budget constraints as well as issues of sample or selection bias. For instance, you fail to mobilize enough respondents to get the desired sample size or a certain demographic compromises an overly large proportion of your sample, thus negatively influencing representativeness. In this part, you should be critical of the weaknesses of your study. Do not try to whitewash them. Being critical proves that you have a solid knowledge of your research design. Meanwhile, take credit by stating how you minimize the impacts of the limitations, and how your study still yields valid and valuable results despite these limitations.

4) Concluding summary. At last, you may close the Methodology section with a concise concluding summary. In this part, you'll want to briefly sum up what you've stated in the section. Here, you can use a figure to wrap up the major design decisions, particularly if a specific model is recommended by your university. Remember this part must be brief, including only a paragraph or two maximum. And keep in mind that your concluding summary includes only what you've already discussed in your section instead of any new information.

4.4 Writing the Discussion

4.4.1 Discussion in Scientific Writing: What and Why

In a dissertation or research paper, the Discussion section is vital and one of the hardest parts to write, and sometimes the longest. The purpose of the Discussion section is to interpret and describe the significance of your findings in light of what was already known about the research problem being investigated and to explain any new understanding or insights that emerged as a result of your study of the problem. The Discussion section will always connect to the Introduction section by way of the research questions or hypotheses you posed and the literature you reviewed, but the Discussion section does not simply repeat or rearrange the first parts of your paper; it clearly explains how your study advanced the reader's understanding of the research problem from where you left them at the end of your review of prior research.

The Discussion section is often considered the most important part of your research paper because this is where you:

- most effectively demonstrate your ability as a researcher to think critically about an issue, to develop creative solutions to problems based on a logical synthesis of the findings, and to formulate a deeper, more profound understanding of the research problem under investigation;
- present the underlying meaning of your research, note possible implications in other areas of study, and explore possible improvements that can be made to further develop the concerns of your research;
- highlight the importance of your study and how it can contribute to understanding the research problem within the field of study;
- state how the findings from your study revealed and helped fill the gap in the literature that had not been previously exposed or adequately described;
- engage the reader in thinking critically about issues based on an evidence-based interpretation of findings; it is not governed strictly by objective reporting of information.

Try to beware of these common mistakes when writing your Discussion section:

- Simply repeating the Results section, with little reference to current literature;
- Making conclusions that the data cannot support—you should learn to tell strong findings apart from weak ones. Do not exaggerate your results;
- Paying too much attention to the limitations of the study, which may make readers question the relevance of the work. On the contrary, some may forget to admit the limitations of their study;
- Repeating what was already said in the introduction without connecting it to the results;
- Presenting no conclusions;
- Introducing topics that were not covered by the study's results/findings.

Your Discussion section should demonstrate you understand your findings. It is usually written in the present tense often with subheadings to make it easier to read. You can adopt these strategies to help you compose a successful discussion.

Explain how your findings link to what is already known in the area as well as to what you intended to find. You should mention your introduction and state whether what you discovered was in line with the current literature, or whether it was somehow unexpected or controversial.

If your results were unusual and/or contradictory, you need to explicate why it was so. Did your sampling method lead to it? Or your choice of methodology? Here, ensure you have completely justified your methodological decisions in the Methodology section of your thesis. Unexpected results might be good, but they can also raise more questions from the committee and other readers, so remember that you have all the answers.

Try to demonstrate both sides of your argument, which will earn your conclusions more reliability. Again, somewhere in your Discussion section openly admit the limitations of your study.

Present one or two suggestions for future research or subsequent studies. Be sure to cover all your results, including those statistically insignificant ones. You might also want to revisit your Introduction section here and emphasize studies that have proven related to the interpretation of your findings.

4.4.2　Discussion Writing: Structure and Style

In the Discussion section, you dig into the meaning, significance and relevance of your findings. It should concentrate on explicating and evaluating what you discovered, demonstrating how it links to your literature review and research questions, and arguing for your comprehensive conclusion. To write this section, you should start by reiterating your research problem and concisely summarizing your major findings. Don't just repeat all the data you have already reported—aim for a clear statement of the overall result that directly answers your main research question. Then, you can center your discussion around four main facts:

- Interpretations—what do the results mean?
- Implications—why are the results important?
- Limitations—what can't the results tell us?
- Recommendations—what practical actions or scientific studies should follow?

In your Discussion section, remember that you are supposed to interpret and explicate your findings, so it's significant to convey the meaning of your results to the reader and show exactly how they address your research questions. Different kinds of research require different forms of interpretations, but some typical methods of interpreting the data include:

- identifying correlations, patterns and links among the data;
- discussing whether the findings met your expectations or supported your hypotheses;
- putting your findings in the context of prior research and theory;
- explicating unanticipated findings and evaluating their importance;

- considering possible alternative explanations and making an argument for your position.

Your Discussion section can be organized around major themes, hypotheses or research questions, following the same structure as your Results section. You can also start by emphasizing the most important or unexpected findings. It may be helpful to follow this sequence: (a) mention your research question; (b) present the answer; (c) explain it with relevant results; (d) relate your work to the work of others.

Besides giving your interpretations, remember to link your results back to the academic work that you surveyed in the literature review. The discussion should indicate how your results fit with current knowledge, what new insights they add, and what consequences they bring to theory or practice. Consider these questions:

- Do your findings align with prior research? If so, what do they contribute to it?
- Are your results very different from other studies? If so, why might this be?
- Do the findings support or challenge current theories?
- Are there any practical implications?

Your aim is to tell the reader exactly what your research has brought and why they should care. No research is perfect, and admitting limitations demonstrates your credence. Limi-tations show exactly what can and cannot be concluded from your study, rather than listing your errors. Limitations might be caused by your overall research design, particular methodological choices, or unexpected obstacles that appeared during the research process. You should only refer to limitations directly related to your research objectives, and evaluate how much influence they exerted on attaining the aims of the research. For instance, if your sample size is not big enough or limited to a specific group of people, note that this limits its generalizability. If you met problems when gathering or analyzing data, explain what impact these had on the findings. If there are uncontrollable confounding variables, state the effect these may have had. After noting the limitations, you can restate the validity of your findings to address your research questions.

You can make suggestions, based on the discussion of your findings, for practical implementation or further research. Sometimes you can include the suggestions in the conclusion. The limitations can directly lead to recommendations for further research. You should have concrete ideas for how future work can build on fields that your study failed to solve instead of just saying that more research should be done.

When writing the Discussion section of your dissertation, try to avoid these common mistakes:

- Simply repeating the Results section, with little reference to current literature.
- Making conclusions that the data cannot validate—you should learn to tell strong findings apart from weak ones.
- Do not exaggerate your results.
- Paying too much attention to the limitations of the study, which may make readers

question the relevance of the work. On the contrary, some may forget to admit the limitations of their study.

- Repeating what was already said in the introduction without connecting it to the results.
- Presenting no conclusions.
- Introducing topics that were not covered by the study's results/findings.

4.5

Writing Other Component Parts

4.5.1 Title Writing: Rules and Techniques

The title of an academic paper is one of the most essential components of the entire writing. Titles have two functions: to identify the main topic or the message of the paper and to attract readers. The title will be read by many people. Only a few will read the entire paper, therefore, all words in the title should be chosen with care. Too short a title is not helpful to the potential reader. Too long a title can sometimes be even less meaningful. Remember a title is not an abstract. Neither is it a sentence. Titles are also useful to the writer. A title chosen at the beginning can remind you not to deviate during the writing process, while writing a title at the end of the process can help you check. If you feel it difficult to choose a title, it may be caused by an unclear main idea or point.

Titles for academic papers are often very long, so your title may be two or more lines long. You can break titles into two parts: the main title and the subtitle. When writing a title, you should consider it as a process and not be shy to expand your thinking during that process, as a successful title does not pop up all of a sudden; it needs deliberating and revising.

You should use words or phrases from the essay question in your title. Some key phrases around methods are repeated in essay assignments, and you may use noun forms of these phrases in essay titles: "analyze", "assess", "compare/contrast", "define", "describe", "discuss", "evaluate", "illustrate", "outline", "relate", "summarize". It is also an effective way to ask a question in a title, which helps make the readers feel curious, but it's usually advisable to give the answer in your title.

If you are struggling with a strong title, jot down your topic and keywords from your essay. They describe the main concept or ideas of the entire essay. You may organize these words in a sentence, or sentences, and then convert them into shorter phrases. Most titles have to be written, expanded, and revised again and again. You should make the title as informative as possible and not worry about its lengthiness or wordiness. Reveal your conclusions. Be straightforward and enthusiastic.

In conclusion, a good title shall be accurate, complete, specific and follows certain rules:

- Use the fewest possible words that describe the contents of the paper;
- Avoid waste words like "Studies on", or "Investigations on";
- Use specific terms rather than general ones;
- Use the same key terms in the title as the paper;
- Watch your word order and syntax;
- Avoid abbreviations, jargon and special characters.

4.5.2 Abstract Writing: Structure and Strategies

An abstract is like a summary of your (published or unpublished) paper, usually about a paragraph long. It should report the main story and several vital details of the paper for readers who only read the abstract and should act as an explicit preview for readers who read your entire paper. The goal of an abstract is to convey what was done, why was it done, how was it done, and what was found.

A good abstract is specific and selective:

- Use one or more well-written paragraphs;
- Use introduction/body/conclusion structure;
- State purpose, findings, conclusions and recommendations in that order;
- Make it understandable to a broad audience.

A successful abstract fulfills several purposes: an abstract informs readers of the gist of your paper or article to decide if they will read the entire paper; an abstract makes readers ready to follow the detailed information, analyses, and arguments in your entire paper; and, an abstract impresses readers with main points from your paper. It's also worth remembering that search engines and bibliographic databases use the abstract, as well as the title, to identify key terms for indexing your published paper. So what you include in your abstract and your title is crucial for helping other researchers find your paper or article.

1. The Contents of an Abstract

Most abstracts contain the following types of information:

- the context or background information for your study;
- the general topic under investigation;
- the specific topic of your research;
- the key questions or statement of the problem your study responds to;
- what's known about this question, what prior investigation has been conducted or found;

- the main reason(s), the exigency, the rationale, the goals for your study—Why is it significant to answer these questions?
- your research and/or analytical methods;
- your main findings, results or arguments;
- the significance or implications of your findings or arguments.

The body of your paper will certainly develop and explicate these ideas in a full manner. The proportion of your abstract devoted to each kind of information and the order of that information may differ, according to the nature and genre of your paper. Sometimes, some of this information is implied, instead of stated clearly.

In an abstract, references are usually not cited, as most of your abstract will report what you have investigated in your research, what you have discovered and what you argue in your paper. In the body section, specific literature that informs your research will be cited.

2. When to Write an Abstract

You must write an abstract when composing a thesis, dissertation, research paper, or submitting an article to an academic journal. Although the abstract appears as the first part of your paper, it is advisable not to write your abstract until after you've drafted your entire paper. In this way, you will know what to summarize. The abstract is usually the last thing you compose. It is supposed to be an independent, self-contained text, rather than an excerpt copied from your paper. An abstract alone should be fully understandable to the readers without reading your entire paper or relevant sources.

3. How to Write an Abstract

The easiest way to compose an abstract is to imitate the structure of a paper by comparing it to a smaller version of your research paper. The abstract typically includes the following main elements: aims, methods, results, conclusion and keywords.

1) Aims. First, you may explicitly define the purpose of your research. What practical or theoretical problem does the research address, or what research question do you intend to respond to? You may include some concise background socially or academically relevant to your topic but avoid detailed information. After specifying the problem, report the objective of your research. Use verbs like "investigate", "test", "analyze" or "evaluate" to demonstrate exactly what you plan to do. This part of the abstract can be written in the present or past simple tense, but should never refer to the future, as the research is already complete.

2) Methods. Next, state the research methods that you used to solve your question. This part should directly describe what you did in one or two sentences. It is usually written in the past simple tense as it talks about completed actions. Do not evaluate validity or obstacles here, because the goal is to provide readers with a quick understanding of the overall approach and procedures you adopted, instead of discussing the methodology's strengths and weaknesses.

3) Results. Next, sum up the major research results. This part can be in the present or past simple tense. Some research might be long and complex, so not all results can be included here. Just emphasize the most essential findings that will enable the reader to understand your conclusions.

4) Conclusion. At last, present the main conclusions of your research: what is your answer to the problem or question? The reader should gain clear knowledge of the key point that your study has proved or argued. Conclusions are usually written in the present simple tense. You must briefly indicate important limitations to your research in the abstract, if there are any. This enables readers to precisely assess the credibility and generalizability of your investigation. If your aim was to solve a practical problem, the conclusions may include recommendations for implementation. If relevant, you can concisely make suggestions for further research.

5) Keywords. If your paper is to be published, you must list the keywords at the end of the abstract. They must reference the most vital elements of the research to help potential readers locate your paper when they are conducting literature searches. Notice that some publication manuals, like APA Style, have specific formatting requirements for these keywords.

It can be challenging to squeeze your entire paper into several hundred words, but the abstract is the first and sometimes only section that readers read, so it's essential to write it well. You may follow these strategies.

1) Reverse outline. Not all abstracts will include the same elements. If your research has a different structure (for instance, a humanities paper that supports an argument through thematic chapters), you can compose your abstract through a process of reverse outlining. First, make a list of keywords from every chapter or section, and sum up the central point in one or two sentences, which can draw a road map of your abstract's structure. Next, organize and connect the sentences to demonstrate how the argument develops. The abstract should offer a condensed version of the entire story by only containing information from the main text. Read your abstract again to ensure it explicitly summarizes your argument.

2) Read other abstracts. The most effective method to know the conventions of writing an abstract is to read other relevant abstracts. While doing your literature review, you probably have already read many journal article abstracts, which can be used as a model for structure and style. In addition, many dissertation abstract examples can also be found in thesis and dissertation databases.

3) Write clearly and briefly. A good abstract is short but strong, so every word must count, and every sentence must explicitly convey one key point. Do not use unnecessary filler words or obscure jargon. Make sure that the abstract must be comprehensible to readers unfamiliar with your topic.

4) Focus on your research. The abstract is designed to state the original contributions of your research, so do not discuss others' work here. The academic background can be summarized here in one or two sentences to put your research in context and indicate its relevance to a broader debate, however, specific publications do not need to be mentioned here. Avoid citations in an abstract unless necessary (for instance, if your research directly addresses another study or centers around an important theorist).

5) Check your formatting. If you are composing a paper for a journal, you need to know the specific formatting requirements for the abstract. You should check the guidelines and format your work accordingly. Pay attention to the word limit. If there is no guideline regarding the length of the abstract, write in a maximum of one double-spaced page.

4.5.3 Conclusion Writing: Functions and Structures

As an essential part of the paper, a conclusion gives closure to the reader while reminding the reader of the contents and significance of the paper. It helps the reader step back from the specifics to have the bigger picture of the paper, and it reminds the reader of the main argument. A conclusion clarifies the intent and significance of the paper rather than introducing new ideas. Besides, it can also recommend possible future research on the topic. Offering clarity and insight into the topic, conclusion is one of the most essential components of a paper, so it is often deemed the hardest section of a paper to compose.

1. When to Use a Conclusion

When writing an article, report or essay that puts forward or studies an idea, issue or event, you should write a conclusion. A thesis statement answers the "why" by providing the structure and motivation for the full paper. On the other hand, a conclusion answers the "so what" by illustrating the point of the essay and providing the reader with a solution, question or insight into the subject matter that restates why it matters. In essay writing, many writers dread composing the Conclusion section the most, because all the points discussed have to be squeezed into a tidy small package. How can you impress the reader for the last time while highlighting the importance of your discoveries? You need an effective method. A successful Conclusion section should finally show your reader that you've achieved what you intend to prove.

2. How to Write a Good Conclusion

To compose your Conclusion section and end your essay, you may begin by reiterating your thesis, the central idea of your full paper; it's advisable to remind the reader of the purpose of your essay. After reiterating your thesis in a rephrased way and providing a fresh understanding, you may proceed to restate your supporting points. Collect the key points from every supporting paragraph or individual argument from the essay and then organize these points together to indicate the significance of the ideas. The conclusion should, rather than just summarizing what you wrote, provide a closure with the larger meaning and further possibilities of the topic.

You may follow these steps to write a good conclusion.

1) Reiterate the thesis. A successful conclusion reminds the reader of the main point and the purpose of the essay. But do not repeat the thesis verbatim. Slightly rephrase your argument with the primary point intact.

2) Restate your supporting points. In addition to the restatement of your thesis, its supporting points throughout the paper must also be restated. However, you should sum up the ideas rather than simply repeating the paper's arguments.

3) Connect your opening statement with the closing statement. By going back to the introduction's themes, you can offer the reader a strong sense of conclusion. You may use similar concepts, return to an original scenario or refer to the same imagery.

4) Provide some insight. After reading your conclusion, the reader ought to be left with a solution, an insight, questions for further investigation or a call to action. What are the implications of your argument? Why should the reader care? These questions are to be answered here, leaving your reader with something to ponder over.

3. What to Include in a Conclusion

With an understanding of what an effective conclusion includes, you can consider finer details. Besides reiterating your thesis and summing up your points, what else should the conclusion encompass? These strategies can help you compose a savvy and thought-provoking conclusion.

1) Ask yourself: "So what?" At the beginning of drafting your thesis, it's helpful to ask yourself this question "So what?" or "Why does it matter?"; at the end of an essay, you should also answer the same question to keep yourself in line with the essay's purpose. Then, at your conclusion, you will not worry about having nothing to say.

2) Add perspective. If you've met a great quote in your research that is not yet used in your paper, you may put it in the conclusion. Including a quote from one of your primary or secondary sources can add to your thesis or final thoughts a different hue, which can bring specificity and texture to your full argument.

3) Consider the clincher. At the very end of the essay, you have to create your closing sentence or clincher. When you consider how to compose a good conclusion, the clincher must be a priority. What can you say to guide the reader to a new view on the subject? The last sentence needs to help readers get a sense of closure with a positive note, so your readers are satisfied that they read your paper and that they acquired something worthwhile.

4. What Not to Include in a Conclusion

Remember to avoid several things when composing your conclusion paragraph, because these elements will only cheapen your overall argument.

Here are a few conclusion mishaps to beware of:

- Do not use phrases like "in summary", "in conclusion" or "to sum up". Readers know they are at the end of the essay and they do not need a signpost.

- Avoid simply summing up what has come before. For a short essay, you do not have to restate all of your supporting arguments. Readers will know if you just copied and pasted from elsewhere.

- Do not introduce brand new ideas or evidence, because this will only perplex readers and undermine your arguments. If there is a profound point that you've arrived at in your conclusion and want to include, try placing it in one of your supporting paragraphs.

While your introduction serves as a bridge that connects your readers from their own lives to the "space" of your argument or analysis, your conclusion must help readers return to their daily lives. By following this helpful road map, you learn how to compose a successful conclusion that provides readers with a solution, a call to action, or a sharp insight for further research.

5. Types of Conclusion

Although various sources cite different kinds of conclusions, all of them fulfill one of these three fundamental functions:

1) Summarization. When writing about technical subjects with a more clinical tone, writers often use this style, like in surveys, definitions and reports. As it rephrases the main ideas of the essay, it is usually used in longer papers where writers need to remind readers of the essay's main points. Avoid reflexive references or subjective ideas, such as "I feel" or "in my opinion".

2) Editorialization. When writing about a controversial topic, writers usually use this style. This style integrates the writer's commentary about the subject matter and usually describes his or her engagement in the matter. A conversational tone or an anecdote will be used in this kind of conclusion to capture attention to concerns, interpretations, personal beliefs or feelings.

3) Externalization. When writing about a particular issue as a part of a much more complex subject, writers use an externalized conclusion to offer a transition into a relevant but separate topic that guides readers to further develop the discussion. It is seen as a new introduction that encompasses another thesis entirely, and develops into another potential essay.

A conclusion is your final chance to convince your readers of your point of view and to let them see you as a writer and thinker. The impression you make in your conclusion will shape the impression that your readers are left with after they finish reading the paper.

📖 Review Questions

1. How can you write an introduction for scientific writing?

2. What is scientific literature? What is a literature review?

3. What are the roles and functions of a literature review in scientific research?

4. What is a Methodology section in scientific writing?

5. How can you write a Methodology section for research articles, theses and dissertations respectively?

6. What is the function of a Discussion section for scientific writing?

7. How can you write a Discussion section for scientific writing?

8. What are the functions of the Title, Abstract and Conclusion sections in scientific writing?

9. How can you write the Title, Abstract and Conclusion sections in scientific writing?

5
Chapter

Language Usage in Scientific Writing

Chapter Lead-in: The use of proper language is an essential element in writing scientific papers. Scientists exchange their findings or knowledge through language. If they do not use proper language, they will fail to convey the message. The language of science or scientific papers differs from that of literary works (e.g., novels, drama, poetry). It has its own rules or conventions shared by scientists. In novels or dramas, it is common for writers to use metaphorical, ambiguous, or flowery language to attract readers, but in scientific papers, such language is avoided. The language of science should be formal, straightforward, concise and brief. A scientist who uses complicated, metaphorical or ambiguous sentences may mislead the readers; accordingly, his or her message will not be properly understood by them.

5.1 Scientific Language: Features and Functions

The language used in scientific writing, i.e., the scientific language, is a language modality characterized by its formality and use of symbols and terms of science. It is used for the transmission of specialized or scientific knowledge. It is usually transmitted through written messages and must be supported by reliable sources and scientific-technical demonstrations. Science requires the use of special language codes to differentiate from colloquial language; there is even specialized language for the different scientific disciplines. Each branch of science uses its own jargon or language codes, such as medicine, biology, technology, astronomy, mathematics, physics, etc. However, despite the semantic differences between sciences, there are basic or common characteristics of scientific language. The scientific language uses specific terms about the subject of which it speaks, so much so that the special lexicon used in scientific texts is its main characteristic. This type of language is also characterized by its objectivity, clarity, precision and accuracy. There is no place for personal opinions or feelings. In this way, science avoids ambiguities and misunderstandings.

The terms such as active voice and passive voice refer to the way subjects and verbs are used in sentence construction. In scientific writing, both voices are used to write clear and coherent research articles. Although many scientists overuse the passive voice, most scientific journals (e.g., *Science* and *Nature*) encourage active voice. The main difference between active voice and passive voice lies in the amount of emphasis given to the person or object acting the sentence, versus the amount of emphasis given to the person or object being acted upon.

The use of tenses in a language as versatile as English can be rather confusing. The situation gets even more muddled when you have to decide which tense to use while writing a scientific research paper. In scientific writing, tense usage depends upon the section of the paper being written. Different sections of the IMRAD format warrant the use of different tenses. These variations within tense usage get even finer and more complex depending on which aspect of the research process is being discussed.

In any scientific document, it is the writer's job to efficiently guide the reader through the information, making the reader's job easy. To accomplish this goal, proper grammar is critical to make your point clear and avoid misunderstandings. One essential element of grammar is correct verb use. It is often found that even the best writers use incorrect verb tenses in scientific writing. Verbs are words that describe actions within sentences and are crucial for strong and effective writing. The verb tense (primarily past, present or future) is used by readers to place information relative to the time of occurrence. The meaning of a statement can completely change solely based on the verb tense used.

Determining the correct verb tense to use can be a challenge in scientific writing, particularly when trying to differentiate previously published results from those that you obtained in your current research. Because different sections of a manuscript are used to deliver different types of information to your readers, specific verb tenses are commonly associated with particular sections of your manuscript.

5.1.1 Stylistic Features of Scientific Language

Good technical communication should be accurate, clear, concise, coherent and appropriate. However, these features might be hard to maintain in scientific and technological essays. Science and technology not merely rely heavily on specialized concepts and terminologies, but use statistics and graphics extensively.

1. Accuracy

Accuracy, the meticulous conforming to fact or truth, includes three major aspects. First, document accuracy refers to appropriately covering your topics in proper detail. An accurate document usually has to center around a problem. Document accuracy is often developed by a clarified problem statement and a preliminary outline. These writing tools can help reduce your data in a way that solves a theoretical or practical problem and thus help concentrate your writing effort. Second, stylistic accuracy refers to carefully using language to convey meaning. To describe and analyze your topics effectively, you have to use precise language, including careful use of paragraph and sentence structure and word choice. To gain command of accuracy, you need to study the elements of style and learn to put those elements into use when drafting, revising, editing and proofreading your paper. Third, technical accuracy demands stylistic accuracy, however, it does not rely solely on it. A technically accurate understanding of the subject is a prerequisite for an effective scientific and technological document. Technical accuracy is based on the writer's conceptual command of the subject and its vocabulary, and his or her ability to analyze and process data precisely. In the science and technology field, you must strive hard to master this technical aspect of subject development.

2. Clarity

Clarity, the ease of understanding, is a particular problem in scientific and technological writing. Specialized languages, statistically detailed analyses and complicated conceptual strategies can make technical subjects difficult to understand even when written by experienced writers and read by experts. You can reinforce the clarity of your paper in these ways.

Structural clarity can be promoted at the level of the entire document, which enables the reader to get the big picture. Abstracts and introductions can be used to forecast the purpose and scope of the document. Tables of contents, problem statements and even strategic repetition can also be used to improve structural clarity. Besides, well-designed and placed graphs and tables as well as descriptive titles and frequent subject headings can be used to help clarify information and guide readers to focus on the big picture. Stylistic clarity is strengthened by simple, straightforward language. Remember to use directly worded sentences instead of overloaded sentences or excessive nominalization. Word choice is also a factor in stylistic clarity; in other words, use simple language as much as possible to counterbalance the abstract and specialized terms of science and technology. Contextual clarity, in which the importance, authorization and implications of your work make sense, also helps ease of understanding. Of course, your readers want to know the context of your paper. What propels you to write? What is your purpose? Whose work has influenced yours? What is the structural and intellectual context of your problem? Those questions are answered in introductions and problem statements and your citations and other references.

3. Conciseness

Conciseness is especially valuable to technical fields. Writers often feel like including all that might be related to their subject, instead of only those related to the communication task at hand. In a concise piece of writing merely the needed material is conveyed. To achieve conciseness, at the level of the entire document, you have to narrow down the scope to a manageable problem and response. A clear introduction and a detailed outline can help you control document length and scope. You may identify and cut material unnecessary to support your arguments. Graphics powerfully contribute to conciseness because they eliminate the amount of prose needed to describe objects and processes, synthesize data and show relationships. To achieve conciseness you need careful revising. You should learn about the strategies for avoiding wordiness. Find ways of cutting unnecessary words, sentences and sections from the document.

4. Coherence

Coherence refers to the quality of hanging together and giving the reader an easily followed path. To improve coherence, you can keep your material logically and stylistically consistent, and organize and convey your ideas in specific patterns. Remember to emphasize the connections among the elements of a document. Coherence can greatly increase the reader's ability to understand your material by improving its flow or readability. Coherence is of special value to science and technology documents due to the intrinsic complexity of the subjects.Coherence helps portray the large picture at the level of the entire document, in which you clarify the relations among different sections of the document. Then readers can get a road map to guide them to foresee the content of your paper. To reinforce coherence, you should link various sections of your paper, including abstracts, clear titles, introductions, and problem statements. The paragraph is a most powerful tool of coherence because you organize material into a topic sentence and supporting sentences, pull them together in paragraphs and highlight different forms of conceptual development. You can develop paragraphs partially through the specific approaches of exemplification, analysis, comparison and contrast, definition, enumeration and description. You can also operate transitional devices at the paragraph level to connect sentences and paragraphs.

5. Appropriateness

Ensure your document is appropriate to your writing goals, your audience's purpose of reading it, and the specific institutional contexts in which it is written and read. Appropriateness relies largely on your reader because a reader's understanding or experience dictates the level of comprehension of technical material. For instance, a managerial audience may not be able to understand a fact indicated by a mathematical equation. All scientific writing should also cater to the specific institutional context that promotes its creation. Not merely should it fulfill the writer's and the reader's purposes but cater to the goals and conventions of the institution. In some cases, there are clear institutional goals and conventions. For instance, in large companies, you may often find the specific goals of various documents and the preferred form and style in company correspondence and style manuals. Pay attention to the context of your work. Classwork should be done within the context of the goals of the class as well as the specific assignment. Research reports should be in line with the general goals and specific conventions of the scientific or technical community in which they exist.

5.1.2 Functions of Scientific Language

Language is a mechanism of speech sounds used for daily communication by public users. Language serves as a way of communication and as a way of exchanging ideas and feelings. People can disseminate various messages through language, either for themselves or for others. Based on one's needs, there are about six different functions of language:

1) Informational function of language. The most conspicuous function of language is informative, which is also known as referential. We encounter this function more than other functions in the text. This function of language is used to transfer a message or information about something directly or indirectly.

2) Expressive function of language. The expressive function of a language indicates the emotions, feelings, desires, moods, etc. This kind of language gives us information about the moods or emotions of the subject and informs us of the tone of the sender directly.

3) Directive function of language. This type of function is exerted to draw the attention of others to trigger a reaction from them. This type of language is used to command an order or to ask questions with an interrogative tone.

4) Phatic function of language. This type of function is used to start or stop a discussion as well as to check the connection between a receiver and the sender.

5) Poetic function of language. It is also called an aesthetic function of language. It focuses on the message itself, by using oratorical aspects to demonstrate its beauty. It is not only applied in the text but also commonly used in the form of quotes and sayings.

6) Meta-linguistic function of language. This is the last function which describes the language itself, including the definitions or meanings of words as well as the interpretation of the language.

The scientific language, as a vehicle of science, serves certain very accurate functions. As mentioned before, it is characterized by precision, exactness and objectivity. Its functions include:

- Transmit information—it transmits specific knowledge to the public and meanwhile represents a specific scientific discipline;
- State arguments—it leads to the concrete, analyzing the subject in question and supporting every argument without adornments.

5.2 Words and Sentences in Scientific Writing

5.2.1 Word Usage in Scientific Writing

In reporting and describing research, try to be as accurate as possible. Wherever possible choose the more precise words with unmistakable meanings. Do not use the ambiguous, the faddish, or the worn-out clichés. For the benefit of foreign readers, use standard words in their established meanings.

1. Technical Terms

Technical terms are an essential part of all scientific writing. Each field and specialty usually uses a vocabulary that conveys various specialized concepts in the way of technical language. These special terms convey concentrated meanings that have been established over significant periods of study of a field. The value of specialized terms lies in the fact that each single term contains a mass of information in a condensed manner. Technical terminology is often regarded as a shorthand, a way of achieving semantic depth and precision with as few words as possible. Technical terms often blend readily into formulae and mathematical manipulation.

However, too many technical terms can also undermine the readability and comprehensibility of prose, even for the specialized reader. When applying specialized terminology, you should follow these four principles:

1) Match terminology to the knowledge of the reader. Sometimes an accurate term is used but fails to reach your reader. You must know your reader's level of comprehension. For readers without expertise in your field, you may have to replace specialized terms with more general ones, which means that you may have to sacrifice certain accuracy about your topic.

2) Use terms with consistency. Remember to use the same term for a specific item every time. The reader might be confused if you shift from using weight to using mass when talking about the quantity of an object, if you refer to a tool as a spanner at first and refers to it as a wrench later, or if you shift from Centigrade to the Kelvin scale for measuring temperature.

3) Clearly define or explain unfamiliar terms. If you refer to a specialized term which is not commonly used in your reader, remember to define it clearly, even if the reader is an expert.

4) Make a terminology list when introducing various new terms into your discussion. The list usually comes before your introduction or in an appendix, and it can be of much help the reader who needs to be reminded of the meaning of the term.

2. Biased Language

Try not to use language that might be read as biased based on gender, age, physical ability or ethnic or racial identity. Use inclusive language instead, to avoid unintended stereotypes. Make sure to call people and groups with the labels they prefer.

1) Sexist language. Do not use masculine pronouns ("he", "his" and "him") for generic references that apply to either sex. You can revise with one of the following approaches:

- Use both a masculine and a feminine pronoun, like "him or her" (but avoid "him/her");
- Pluralize the antecedent and the pronoun, with other necessary alterations;
- Rewrite the sentence without using the pronoun.

In most written works it is still unacceptable to use the plural pronoun "their" to address an indefinite singular antecedent, even if it is becoming common in speech. For instance, "every doctor has their specialty". Use words like "humans" or "the human race" rather than "man" and "mankind", and find replacements for occupational designations formed with the word "man". Finally, avoid information that does not necessarily refer to a person's gender, and treat the titles of men and women comparably.

2) Ageist language. "Senior citizens", a general term for the older population, can be interpreted as offensive due to its political connotations. As well, "the elderly" suggests feebleness to some. When referring to this group of people, you should use more specific expressions to include the population or person you have in mind, such as people over sixty-five, retirees or octogenarians. More generically, the expression "older people", although vague, contains nothing negative. Never use disparaging terms or informal ones like "seniors", "old folks" or "golden agers". More importantly, never stereotype older people as physically or mentally enfeebled.

3) Language biased against people with disabilities. When mentioning individuals with specific disabilities, first make sure it is necessary to note the disability. If it is, refer to it in a way that does not define the person by the disability. You can use the terms "disability" and "disabled" instead of "handicap" or "crippled". You may also use more positive euphemisms, such as "physically challenged" and "differently abled". If it is not, do not refer to it at all. Generally speaking, apply terminology that addresses a disability or a disease neutrally instead of negatively.

4) Ethnically or racially biased language. Professional writing certainly does not allow ethnic or racial insults. Less clear-cut labels are most appropriate to refer to specific ethnic and racial communities. Do not use unsupported generalizations about racial or ethnic communities or racially based assumptions about individuals. Refer to ethnicity or race only when relevant. Do not use pronouns that indicate that "we" are of one race and "they" are of another.

5.2.2　Sentences in Scientific Writing

The following are some typical paying-attentions in syntax usage in scientific writing.

1. Wordiness

Conciseness is vital to all writing, scientific writing in particular. So, avoid wordy writing and try to use as few words as possible to express your points without undermining clarity or leaving out important information.

Nominalizations. Wordiness can also be caused by too much or unnecessary nominalization (changing verbs into nouns), because it needs a noun and a verb rather than just the verb form.

So use verb forms where possible.

Unnecessary repetition. A most common kind of superfluous repetition pertains to modifiers repeating information contained by the word modified. So, eliminate unnecessary repetition.

Unnecessary words and phrases. In sentences, every word and phrase must help the meaning and clarity. You should avoid these two frequently used sentence structures "There is/ are ..." and "It is ..." Delete redundant material when revising your first draft.

2. Modifiers

Modifiers are usually optional elements of sentences, such as adjectives, adverbs, adjective clauses, and adverbial clauses. And they should change the interpretation or meaning of the words or phrases they modify.

Stacked modifiers. Do not use a long chain of modifiers or nouns. It is difficult to read these strings of modifiers and nouns, which sometimes may be ambiguous. You may add a few words, conjunctions and prepositions in particular to make the links between nouns understandable to the audience.

Misplaced modifiers. To achieve clarity, modifiers must be placed with care. Modifiers should be placed in a way that they do not interrupt the sentence structure or cause ambiguity.

Modifiers of nouns. Modifiers of nouns should be placed either right before or right after the noun. If another phrase splits the noun and its modifier, the modifier may be mistaken as modifying a noun in the separating phrase instead of the original noun.

Adverb modifiers. Adverbs must be put as close as possible to the words or phrases that they modify. If an adverb is separated from the word or phrase that it applies to, the adverb might be ambiguously misinterpreted. And always put a quantity adverb right before the word it applies to. Pay special attention to the placement of the adverbs "only" and "just". To move the adverb cannot merely cause ambiguity to the meaning of a sentence but bring drastic change to it.

Dangling modifiers. A dangling modifier refers to one connected to the sentence in an implied, intended but not explicit way. Because dangling modifiers worsen the clarity of your writing, your modifiers must be appropriately joined with the words they modify. To fix a dangling modifier, you should add the word or phrase the modifier is supposed to modify and rearrange the sentence.

3. Agreement

Agreement between subjects and verbs and between pronouns and their antecedents is essential for paragraph coherence and style and grammar. When editing your essay, you should pay due attention to agreement between subjects and verbs, as well as pronouns and their antecedents: a) Check if the subject agrees with its verb (subject-verb agreement);

b) Check if the pronouns agree in gender and number with their antecedents (pronoun-antecedent agreement); c) Check if the form of the pronoun is proper for how it is used in the sentence (pronoun case); d) For clarity, check if the pronouns are closely connected with their antecedents (pronoun reference).

Subject-verb agreement. There is agreement in number and person between the verb and its subject. In other words, a singular subject has a singular verb, and a plural subject goes together with a plural verb; the first-person subject requires the first-person verb, while a subject in the second or third person calls for its appropriate verb. Generally speaking, when writing with present tense verbs and nouns without irregular plural forms, you can simply think of subject-verb agreement as using one -s per clause, either on the subject or on the verb, but not on both. Be careful not to be confused by modifying phrases between the subject and the verb. If you are not clear about the subject-verb agreement, check the sentence by cutting the modifiers.

Collective nouns involve groups, like committee (group of people), flock, (group of birds) or herd (group of animals). If a collective noun serves as the subject of your sentence, you have to be extra careful about subject-verb agreement. Use a singular verb when the collective noun refers to the individuals acting as one unit. Use a plural verb when the collective noun is interpreted as individuals acting separately. If you are emphasizing individual members of a collective noun, the best way is by adding the word "members".

With two or more nouns comprising the subject, special attention needs to be paid to subject-verb agreement. If the coordinating conjunction "and" connects the nouns, a plural verb should be used. On the other hand, a singular verb should be used, if the nouns are conventionally regarded as one item. If the coordinating conjunction "or" connects the nouns, agreement should be made between the verb and its nearer noun. If the correlative conjunction "both ... and" connects the nouns, a plural verb should be used. If the correlative conjunctions "either ... or", "neither ... nor" or "not only ... but also" connect the nouns, the verb should be in agreement with the nearer noun.

Pronoun-antecedent agreement. A pronoun should agree with its antecedent in gender and number. If required, carefully choose pronouns to eliminate sexist language. In some cases, the best solution to avoid sexist language is to change the singular to the plural. When the antecedent is a singular indefinite pronoun, a singular pronoun should be used to refer to it. In such cases, you should choose appropriate pronouns to avoid sexist language. An effective way is to change the singular to the plural. When the antecedent is a plural indefinite pronoun, a plural pronoun should be used to refer to it. If the coordinating conjunction "and" joins the antecedents, a plural pronoun should be used. If the coordinating conjunctions "or" and "nor" join the antecedents, agreement in gender and number should be made between the pronoun and its closest antecedent. If antecedents follow "each" or "every", a singular pronoun should be used. Here is a special case. If a plural antecedent precedes "each", a plural pronoun should be used.

When a collective noun acts as a group, a singular pronoun should be used to refer to it. When a collective noun acts as individual, a plural pronoun should be used to refer to the members.

Pronoun case. A pronoun can appear in one of the three cases: a) subjective, in which the pronoun acts as a subject; b) objective, in which the pronoun acts as an object; and c) possessive, in which the pronoun acts as a possessor. If you are uncertain which pronoun form to use after a coordinating conjunction, test the pronoun alone in the sentence, without the conjunction. If you are uncertain which pronoun form to use after a coordinating conjunction, avoid using a reflexive pronoun. Test the pronoun alone in the sentence, without the conjunction. Use objective pronouns as subjects of infinitives. Use possessive pronouns with gerunds. Use "whom" as an object and "who" as a subject. It is commonly accepted in informal contexts to use "who" for both subjects and objects, but in formal writing, "whom" should be used for the objective case.

Pronoun reference. Pronoun reference involves the identification of a pronoun with its intended antecedent. In pronoun reference, two problems are commonly seen: a) unclear pronoun reference. You can use a pronoun to refer to the intended antecedent, only when there is a strong connection between them. Between your pronoun and its intended antecedent, clear other nouns with the same gender and number. Otherwise, your pronoun reference may be ambiguous. b) broad pronoun reference. You can use a demonstrative pronoun only when the connection to the intended antecedent of the pronoun is strong enough. Otherwise, your pronoun reference might be too broad, and thus unclear. Check whether all of your pronouns can be easily identified.

Indefinite pronouns. Use singular verbs with indefinite pronouns such as "nobody", "somebody", "anybody", "everybody", "no one", "someone", "anyone", "everyone", "nothing", "something", "anything", and "everything".

4. Sentence Structure

Overloaded sentences. If the audience finds it difficult to follow the sentences which include too much information, you should split such sentences into more easily understandable pieces.

Sentence fragments. A sentence fragment refers to an incomplete but punctuated sentence, with a subject, a verb, or both missing. To fix a sentence fragment, you may add the missing element (subject or verb), or combine the fragment with a clause that contains a subject and a verb. When editing your documents, make sure that there is no sentence fragment.

Comma splice. A comma alone cannot be used to link two separate clauses. The following four ways can help correct a comma splice error: a) Divide the clauses into two independent sentences. Punctuate both sentences with periods. b) Replace the comma with a semicolon or with a semicolon and a conjunctive adverb like "however" or "furthermore". (The conjunctive adverb is also usually followed by a comma.) c) Replace the comma with a coordinating conjunction. d) Change one of the clauses into a subordinate clause.

Fused sentences. Avoid two separate clauses running together without a conjunction or punctuation between them. This mistake is called a fused sentence. The tips under comma splice can help join two independent clauses.

Stringy sentences. Do not string clauses, if dividing them into separate clauses contributes to readability and comprehensibility.

Sentences beginning with "there". If you start the sentence with "there" and the verb precedes the subject, you need to be extra careful about subject-verb agreement. If the noun following "there" is singular, the verb should also be singular. If the noun following "there" is plural, the verb should be plural, as well.

Choppy sentences. Do not use too many short sentences which might create choppy prose. Use various sentence types and connect short related sentences by creating dependent clauses or phrases.

Interrupted sentence structure. The placement of a modifier between the subject and the verb or between the verb and its direct object may weaken the structure of the sentence and make the sentence difficult to read. Generally speaking, the longer and more complex the modifier, the more it worsens the sentence. If possible, do not put a modifier between the verb and its direct object. If possible, do not separate an infinitive with a modifier inserted between the verb and "to".

5. Parallelism and Comparison

Lack of parallelism. Parallelism requires parts of a sentence with the same function to be the same in structure. In other words, words or phrases connected by coordinating conjunctions should have the same form. Phrases connected by coordinating or correlative conjunctions must be parallel. That is to say, all phrases must be of the same type. All items or phrases in lists must be parallel. All headings and subheadings must be parallel with the other headings and subheadings of the same level. All entries of the same level in an outline must be parallel.

Nonparallel comparisons. When you make a comparison, you must ensure the two items parallel in structure.

Faulty comparisons. Comparison can be a very effective way to describe an object or a process. However, to create a powerful comparison, you should keep parallelism, include the basis of your comparison, and avoid ambiguity in your comparison.

Incomplete comparisons. To be complete, a comparison must contain both the item being compared and the item it is being compared with. If the item being compared with is missing, the audience may not get your intended point. Thus, incomplete comparisons sag the clarity of your writing.

Ambiguous comparisons. When describing a comparison, you can shorten the basis of it to avoid wordiness. But make sure that you abbreviate your bases of comparison carefully; otherwise, it can lead to ambiguity. So remember to check whether the basis is still clear after you shorten it. You may add a pronoun to fix an ambiguous comparison and add an auxiliary verb to fix ambiguous comparisons.

6. Tense

Sequence of tenses. Choose the exact tenses of verbs to describe the timing or order of events that you are stating. Usually, the specific order of events being described will need you to apply different verb tenses within a single sentence or paragraph. It is proper to change your verb tenses based on the actual sequence of the events, but you should avoid any unnecessary switch in tenses. Be careful about how you describe the sequence of tenses when stating the timing of events or when rephrasing ideas.

Sequence of tenses and timing of events. A form of the perfect auxiliary "have" can be used to state that an event happened or was finished before another event. The present perfect tense can be applied to describe states or actions that happened at an unknown past time, were repeated in the past, or started at an unspecified time in the past and continue into the present. The present perfect must contain the present tense form of the auxiliary "have" and the past participle of the following verb. The perfect often involves the following adverbs such as "already", "always", "ever", "for", "just", "lately", "never", "recently", "since", "still", and "yet". A present participle can be used to describe that an event in a participial phrase happened at the same time as the event described in the main clause. To emphasize that an event in a participial phrase occurred before the event described in the main clause, use a perfect auxiliary and a past participle. When writing formal documents, use the simple past tense to describe habitual actions. The modal "would" is often used to indicate past tense habitual actions, but it is usually used in spoken and informal contexts.

Sequence of tenses and paraphrasing. When paraphrasing a written idea, introduce the paraphrase with a present tense verb (e.g., "writes") and avoid changing the original verb tenses of the idea. When paraphrasing an ongoing or future spoken idea, introduce the paraphrase with a present or future tense verb (e.g., "says") and avoid changing the original verb tenses of the idea. When paraphrasing a previously spoken idea, introduce the paraphrase with a past tense verb (e.g., "said") and change the verb tenses of the idea to match the tense of that verb. If a previously spoken idea is a common fact that always holds true or concerns a future event that has not happened yet, you can either maintain the original verb tenses of the idea or switch them to past tense to match the tense of the verb you used to introduce the idea. Keeping the original tense highlights the continuing validity of the idea, while switching the verb tenses singles out the narrative quality of the paraphrase.

7. Inappropriate Shift

Keep consistent in your choice of tense, mood, person, and voice. If you cannot justify the shift, do not switch any of them. Otherwise, it will worsen the clarity of your writing.

Inappropriate shifts in tense. Keep consistent in verb tenses within a sentence or a paragraph. An unjustifiable shift in tense can distort the order of events being described and will perplex your audience. For instance, if you use a verb in the past tense to start a description, do not shift to a verb in the present tense.

Inappropriate shifts in mood. Keep consistent in your choice of mood. An unjustifiable switch in mood will perplex your audience. For instance, avoid combining an imperative clause with an indicative clause in one sentence. If you start a description in the conditional (often seen as a variety of the subjunctive), avoid shifting to the indicative.

Inappropriate shifts in person. Keep consistent in your choice of person. An unjustifiable switch in person will perplex your audience. For instance, if you begin a description in the first person, avoid shifting to the second person.

Inappropriate shifts in voice. Keep consistent in your choice of voice. An unjustifiable switch in voice will perplex your audience. For instance, avoid combining a passive voice clause with an active voice clause in one sentence.

8. Voices

When the passive voice is inappropriate, you should use the active voice, instead. Usually active verbs contribute to brief prose, while sentences with passive verbs need more words. Furthermore, passive verbs weaken or completely omit the performer of the action of the verb.

9. Quantifiers

Quantifiers are composed of "all", "most", "many", "more", "some", "none", "few", "both", "each", "every", etc. Some quantifiers are singular, some are plural, and some may be either. When the subject contains a quantifier, be careful about choosing a proper verb. When an uncountable (mass) noun is modified by a quantifier, a singular verb must be chosen. A plural verb must be used when a countable noun is modified by one of the following quantifiers such as "all", "most", "many", "some", "few", "both". When a quantifier is followed by "of", the verb must be in agreement in number with the noun that follows the quantifier. The quantifiers such as "one", "each" and "every" usually require singular verbs, whether followed by "of" or not. A singular verb should be used after a coordinate noun phrase (two or more nouns connected by a coordinating conjunction like "and") beginning with "each" or "every". Here is a special case. A plural verb should be used, when "each" follows a plural noun or pronoun or a compound subject (two or more nouns or pronouns connected by the coordinating conjunction "and").

5.3　Paragraphs in Scientific Writing

Paragraphs are used to highlight important ideas within a piece of writing. They usually involve several sentences that support one central idea. All sentences in a paragraph should discuss the same topic or major theme. That is, the main sentence, supporting information, and ending sentence should all center on a single concept. Paragraphs help readers understand the text by dividing it into small sections. Each section can be read as a complete unit that makes sense independently from other parts of the text. This allows readers to jump back and forth between paragraphs for greater flexibility. Also, paragraphs are used to organize content within documents because they provide a natural division of topics without requiring any additional tags.

A successful paragraph should always include the following four elements: unity, coherence, a topic sentence, and enough development. Paragraphs should have both coherence and unity.

5.3.1　Paragraph Unity and Paragraph Coherence

A paragraph with unity extensively develops a single idea and connects it to the rest of the paper. Paragraph coherence is achieved when sentences are organized logically and when clear transitions connect them.

1. Paragraph Unity

Paragraphs with unity can be difficult to write because they must explore one topic without wandering too far from it. The best paragraphs bring together information from different sources to provide a complete picture of the subject. They may describe how several things relate to each other or give an overview of a broad topic area. Paragraphs with unity are important for essays because they help the reader understand the connection between the parts of an essay, as well as the whole.

Unify paragraphs by making every sentence support the main idea, which is usually stated in a topic sentence. A topic sentence is crucial to a coherent and unified paragraph, because it states the central idea of the paragraph, and the other sentences support it with relevant information and evidence. The topic sentence may be placed anywhere in a paragraph, however, it is the first sentence in most cases. It may also include a transition from the preceding paragraph.

2. Paragraph Coherence

A coherent paragraph not merely lays down the facts but also organizes them and creates a logical argument that flows smoothly from one idea to another. Coherent paragraphs consist of a beginning, a middle, and an end. The elements which improve coherence include transitional devices, linking pronouns, and repetition of keywords.

Transitional devices are key elements to paragraph coherence because they act as verbal "bridges" that connect idea to idea, fill gaps between abrupt, choppy sentences and help create seamless prose. You should use transitional devices to smooth the flow from one idea to another. Here are some examples of frequently used transitional words and phrases according to different types of relationships:

- Cause and effect: consequently, therefore, accordingly, as a result, because, for this reason, hence, thus
- Sequence: furthermore, in addition, moreover, first, second, third, finally, again, also, and, besides, further, in the first place, last, likewise, next, then, too
- Comparison or contrast: similarly, also, in the same way, likewise, although, at the same time, but, conversely, even so, however, in contrast, nevertheless, nonetheless, notwithstanding, on the contrary, otherwise, still, yet
- Example: for example, for instance, in fact, indeed, of course, specifically, that is, to illustrate
- Purpose: for this purpose, for this reason, to this end, with this object
- Time or location: nearby, above, adjacent to, below, beyond, farther on, here, opposite to, there, to the south, before, after, later, afterward, immediately, in the meantime, meanwhile, now, since, soon, then, while

When referring to other nouns or pronouns, you may use linking pronouns, such as "its", "your", and "their", to link your sentences and help focus your subject. You can highlight your major points by deliberately repeating the keywords. Be careful that excessive repetition may cause monotony.

5.3.2 Paragraph Development

You should develop paragraphs in various patterns that appropriately manifest your thinking about the material. When writing the topic sentence and its supporting sentences, you should consider ways to structure your thinking, such as a chronological narration of events, an analysis of the topic, or a physical description. These modes of paragraph development often appear during the process of revision. You can use more than one mode in a series of paragraphs.

The following are some useful patterns of paragraph development.

1) Exemplification. Exemplification paragraphs can give examples to clarify the topic sentence.

2) Narration. Narration follows a chronological pattern of development, and informs the audience of a series of events that occurred. It helps convince the reader because it tells a coherent story and is often easily understandable.

3) Process. To describe how an action is conducted or how something works, you may apply the process in paragraphs to establish sequences. A stricter process description contains more technical terminology, which might be experimental protocol.

4) Description. Descriptive prose identifies the shapes, materials, positions, and functions of its subject and presents a physical picture or a functional view of the subject. Physical descriptive prose usually acts as the raw material for analytical prose.

5) Comparison and contrast. Comparison and contrast examine similarities or differences between the subject and another thing, process, or state. The comparison focuses on the similarities, while contrast, the dissimilarities. Both of them can be used in a single paragraph.

6) Analogy. Analogy is used to illustrate that one object or process is a reference to another. You have to be able to judge whether an analogy is effective. For instance, comparing an apple to the space shuttle probably does not make a valid analogy; whereas, illustrating the Internet in terms of a highway system may have more validity.

7) Cause and effect. As an analytical mode of paragraph development, cause and effect demonstrate the linkage of causation. In other words, how events are caused or influenced by others. When you want to track the occurrence of one event or situation out of another, you may apply cause and effect in paragraphs.

8) Classification and division. Classification and division help you relate parts to the whole. In classification, you group similar things or processes into classes. In other words, you can categorize mechanisms, organisms, and processes according to shapes, magnitudes, effects, etc. In division, you split a topic into smaller parts. Classification is the tutorial prose strategy because it effectively demonstrates the terrain of a subject by its key types.

9) Definition. Defining is a useful way of controlling the scope of terms. You can develop paragraphs by definition when you intend to establish working generalizations that can control the meaning and scope of major terms.

10) Analysis. If you intend to examine a subject, you may analyze it by evaluating one of its aspects, such as weighing evidence and possible causal linkages. There are many resemblances between analysis and other forms of paragraph development, classification and division in particular. Analysis aims to delve into the center of how something functions.

11) Enumeration. Enumeration is an effective approach to set a series of observations and highlight every element. So you may apply enumeration in paragraphs when you intend to list or itemize a set of topics or a series of some sort.

Review Questions

1. What are the features and functions of scientific language?

2. What are the strategies of word usage in scientific writing?

3. What are the syntax rules and principles in scientific writing?

4. What are the modes of paragraph development in scientific writing?

5. What is paragraph unity in scientific writing?

6. What is paragraph coherence in scientific writing?

6
Chapter

Databases, Grey Literature and Searching Strategies

Learning Objectives

After reading this chapter, you should be able to:

1. Know about the typical academic research databases used in scientific research;

2. Know how to use academic research databases for scientific research;

3. Understand grey literature and know how to search for grey literature for scientific research.

Chapter Lead-in: Systematic reviews aid the analysis and dissemination of evidence, using rigorous and transparent methods to generate empirically attained answers to focused research questions. Identifying all evidence relevant to the research questions is an essential component and challenge of systematic reviews. A systematic review search includes a search of databases, gray literature, personal communications, and a hand search of high-impact journals in the related field. A comprehensive literature search cannot be dependent on a single database, nor on bibliographic databases only. The inclusion of multiple databases helps avoid publication bias (geographic bias or bias against the publication of negative results).

6.1 Academic Research Databases and Searching Strategies

Research databases provide access to published magazines and scholarly journal articles you will generally not find freely on the Internet. There are dozens of amazing databases online that can help if you're unsure what's available. Many of them provide access to peer-reviewed articles on all types of topics, and you can often search based on detailed filters and keywords. The search terms (keywords) you use are extremely important. Databases are structured in similar ways and have common features. This means that if you can search one database effectively, then your skills are transferable to other databases. You will need search techniques to find articles in any research database.

6.1.1 Typical Academic Research Databases

Whether writing a thesis, dissertation, or research paper, you have to survey previous literature and research findings from reliable resources, especially peer-reviewed research articles. With academic research databases, it is easier for you to find the literature you are searching for.

An academic research database is a collection of information, used for research and writing. It provides access to scholarly journals. Meanwhile, it also contains many content directories, such as articles, images, scientific papers, and market trend reports. Thus, only by entering certain keywords for research papers can you identify a large number of useful journal articles. Usually, you can read these articles online. Whereas, you have to pay in some cases.

Research papers must be precise and error-free, so you should refer to high-quality academic papers or journals to ensure the accuracy of the paper. In this way, academic research databases provide the ideal way for research paper writing because they can offer you reliable, precise, and latest research information in a time-saving and energy-saving way.

Numerous databases may be used for academic research. Some typical and popular databases are listed below.

1. Scopus

Scopus is the biggest abstract and citation database of peer-reviewed literature, including scientific journals, books and conference proceedings. Scopus provides a comprehensive overview of the world's research output, featuring smart tools to track, analyze and visualize research. As one of the two big commercial, bibliographic databases, Scopus covers scholarly literature from almost any discipline, including science, technology, medicine, social sciences, and arts and humanities. In addition to searching for research articles, Scopus also delivers academic journal rankings, author profiles, and an h-index calculator.

2. Web of Science

Web of Science, formerly called Web of Knowledge, is a database of bibliographic citations of multidisciplinary areas, such as medical, scientific, and social sciences including humanities. Thomson Reuters (Thomson Scientific) set it up in 2004 as a part of Thomson Cooperation, to integrate the citation indices and provide a scope for analysis of indexing and citations. It demands a commercial subscription and helps in viewing the references. It is also used to search a subject and cited references; for example, it retrieves the articles cited by a reference article and helps view the references cited in a related article. It shows 10 to 15 results per page, with details including the names of the authors and the sources. The articles can be searched by using entries like author name, country, title, and source. This database benefits in retrieving many articles from different disciplines in a time-saving manner. Web of Science is the second largest bibliographic database. Academic institutions usually give free access to either Web of Science or Scopus on their campus network.

3. PubMed

As a free resource, PubMed is designed to improve both global and personal health. It helps search and retrieve biomedical and life sciences literature. The PubMed database includes over 34 million citations and abstracts of biomedical literature. Although it does not contain full-text journal articles; it usually presents links to the full text if available from other sources, like the publisher's website or PubMed Central (PMC). PubMed became available online to the public in 1996 and was developed and is maintained by the National Center for Biotechnology Information (NCBI), at the U.S. National Library of Medicine (NLM), located at the National Institutes of Health (NIH).

4. ERIC

ERIC (Education Resources Information Center) is an authoritative database of indexed and full-text education literature and resources. Financially supported by the Institute of Education Sciences of the U.S. Department of Education, it is a crucial tool for education researchers of all kinds. For education sciences, ERIC is the number one destination.

5. IEEE Xplore

In the field of engineering and computer science, IEEE Xplore is the leading academic database, including not only journal articles but conference papers, standards and books. The IEEE Xplore digital library provides the access to reliable research, like journals, conferences, standards, eBooks and educational courses. It contains over 5 million documents that help ignite the imagination, build from prior research, and enlighten fresh ideas.

6. ScienceDirect

As Elsevier's premier full-text platform, ScienceDirect collects high-quality publications with cutting-edge technology and intuitive tools to benefit teaching, coursework and research with more efficiency and effectiveness. ScienceDirect is home to a large number of highly respected journals and prestigious society titles, and provides a vital information resource to more than 15,000,000 scientists all over the world. It is the gateway to the millions of academic articles published by Elsevier. And 2,500 journals and over 40,000 e-books can be searched via a single interface.

7. Directory of Open Access Journals (DOAJ)

DOAJ (Directory of Open Access Journals) was launched in 2003 with 300 open-access journals. Today, this independent index contains approximately 17,500 peer-reviewed, open-access journals covering all areas of science, technology, medicine, social sciences, arts and humanities. Open-access journals from all countries and in all languages are allowed for indexing. DOAJ is sponsored by many libraries, publishers and other organizations with common interests. The DOAJ is a very special academic database, for all the articles indexed are freely and openly accessible.

8. JSTOR

As a digital library, JSTOR provides access to over 12 million journal articles, books, images, and primary sources in 75 disciplines. JSTOR is part of ITHAKA, a non-profit organization that also includes Artstor, Ithaka S+R, and Portico. JSTOR is another essential resource to identify research papers. Any article published before 1924 in the U.S. is available free of charge and JSTOR provides scholarships for independent researchers, as well.

9. EBSCO

EBSCO is the major provider of research databases, e-journal and e-package subscription management, book collection development and acquisition management, and a leading provider of library technology, e-books and clinical decision solutions for universities, colleges, hospitals, corporations, government, K12 schools and public libraries all over the world. From research, acquisition management, subscription services and discovery for clinical decision support and patient care, learning, and research and development, EBSCO provides libraries, healthcare and medical institutions, corporations and government agencies with access to content and resources to meet the information and workflow demands of their users and organizations.

10. ProQuest Dissertation & Theses Global (PQDT) Database

The ProQuest Dissertation & Theses Global (PQDT) database is the world's most comprehensive curated collection of multi-disciplinary dissertations and theses all over the world, providing more than 5 million citations and approximately 3 million full-text works from thousands of universities. There is a wealth of scholarship within dissertations and theses, however, it does not receive due attention because most are unpublished.

11. Springer

Springer is a leading worldwide scientific, technical and medical portfolio, offering researchers in academia, scientific institutions and corporate R&D departments with quality content through innovative information, products and services. Springer hosts one of the most powerful STM and HSS eBook collections and archives, as well as a comprehensive range of hybrid and open-access journals and books under the SpringerOpen imprint. Springer is part of Springer Nature, a global publisher that serves and supports the research community. Springer Nature aims to promote discovery by publishing robust and insightful science, assisting the development of new areas of research and making ideas and knowledge accessible throughout the world.

12. Wiley Online Library

Boasting one of the world's most extensive multidisciplinary collections of online resources covering life, health and physical sciences, social sciences, and the humanities, Wiley Online Library delivers seamless integrated access to more than 4 million articles from 1,500 journals, 9,000 books, hundreds of multi-volume reference works, lab protocols and databases. Featuring a clean and easy-to-use interface, this online service provides an intuitive navigation, enhanced discoverability, expanded functionalities and a range of personalization and alerting options.

6.1.2 Techniques for Searching Literature in Academic Research Databases

As one of the most creative aspects of research, searching is a process of discovery that may increase your knowledge and widen your views. A literature search collects present knowledge or data around a topic or research question, which helps cultivate a basic understanding of a topic of interest, support the thesis/argument of an academic paper or presentation, explicate the need for further research in a specific subject field, summarize/synthesize present evidence relevant to a specific research question, make evidence-informed decisions in a clinical setting.

Although the purpose of a literature search may vary, all searches follow some basic steps in the search process.

Step 1: Identifying the Words to Search for

Begin by laying out your research question. First, filter out the words that will not be useful for your search. Because search engines search for exactly what you type into them, including words like "the", you must make sure you only use the keywords which represent your main concepts.

Mark the words that tell you what to do with the information once you've located it, evaluated it and considered it. They're related to the writing you will do later. You don't need them now.

Underline any limits in the question. Some examples of these are: geographical locations, periods in history, demographic groups, specific types of clinical tests, or the date range for the literature you are searching. These can help you improve your search. Some of these limits will be used as keywords. Some will be filters in a database.

Now take a look at the left words. Emphasize the words and phrases that represent the key concepts you are searching for information on. Draw a table and write the word or phrase for one concept at the top of each column.

If you know of any alternate ways of stating a concept, write those underneath that concept, including alternate spellings and acronyms, e.g., "impact", "consequences" and "repercussions" for "effect", "computer modeling" and "computer simulation" for "computer modeling". It does not matter if no alternate words come to you at this stage. And you will find more as you search. It is just a beginning. If studying health and medical sciences, you will have to consider the MeSH terms for your keywords, as well.

Step 2: Formatting the Words for Searching

After deciding the key concepts you need to search for information on, you can use the following techniques to maximize the potential of each of the words and phrases:

1) **Phrase searching.** In searching, a phrase refers to a group of two or more words that represent an idea. When searching for a phrase, use double quotation marks around the words, e.g., "ozone layer". This instructs the database to look for occurrences of this given group of words in exactly this order.

2) **Truncation.** If a word has different forms, you can add a truncation symbol to the root word, e.g., "pollut*" will search for "pollution", "pollute", "pollutes", "polluter", "polluters", "polluted", "polluting", "pollutant", "pollutants". It's the simplified version of pollution OR pollute OR pollutes OR polluter OR polluters OR polluted OR polluting OR pollutant OR pollutants. Truncation symbols vary slightly between databases, if you are uncertain, use the "Help" or "Search Tips" options to check which one is appropriate.

3) **Wildcards.** There may be variations in the spelling of words, e.g., British English and American English have different spellings for some words. If you search with only one spelling, you will miss the related results with the alternate spelling. You can use the symbol of a wildcard character to replace a letter within a word, e.g., "organi?ation" will search for both "organisation" and "organization". Wildcard symbols vary slightly between databases, so use the "Help" or "Search Tips" options to check which one is appropriate.

4) **Plural terms.** Check how the database you are using searches for single/plural versions of keywords, because this may have an enormous impact on your results. Some databases will automatically search for the plural version of a singular term, but not the reverse (this information is usually included under "Help" or "Search Tips").

Step 3: Turning the Words into Searches

Keywords can be formatted and combined into searches using specific words and symbols. You can use these techniques to maximize the effectiveness of your searches and achieve better quality results.

AND—is used to combine words for different concepts, e.g., "ozone layer" AND pollution". It tells the database to identify results where all forms of the words appear, which narrows your search.

OR—is used to add synonyms or similar concepts to the search. It tells the database to identify results where one of the words or phrases appears, e.g., effect OR impact OR consequences OR repercussions, which widens your search.

NOT—is used to exclude terms you do not intend to find, which narrows your search.

Brackets ( )—are used when you are using both AND and OR in a basic search. Because there is only one search box in a basic search, brackets are needed to group the synonyms that are combined using OR. The other words that have been combined with AND are placed outside the brackets, e.g., (effect OR impact OR consequences OR repercussions) AND "ozone layer" AND pollution. This tells the database to identify at least one of the words or phrases from within the brackets as well as all of the words outside the brackets. It is a way of doing multiple searches at the same time.

Step 4: Using the Filters and Limits in Databases to Refine Your Search

Most databases offer a range of options that enable you to improve your search results by controlling particular elements of your search. Although every database has its options for improving the search, most databases have the following common options:

1) Basic limits. Usually near the top of the menu, there are basic limits that just require you to tick a checkbox, or select/enter dates. They usually include: publication date, peer-reviewed content, and type of publication.

2) Article type. Certain databases permit you to narrow down your search to a particular type of document, for instance: academic journal articles, case studies, conference papers, technical papers, reports, and review articles.

3) Specific fields. All databases categorize information about their documents into specific fields, which can be used for conducting more accurate searches. Enter the Advanced Search, and you can see a drop-down list of available fields next to every search box. Put your words into the box and select the field you intend to search for them in. The following are examples of searchable fields:

- Author.
- Title—this is the article title.
- Subject.
- Abstract—this is the summary of the article.
- Title, abstract and keywords.
- All except full text—this is all fields of the record but not the full article. It includes the abstract.
- Publication name—this is the journal title.

Step 5: Reviewing Your Search Results

Review your search results during and after your searches, which helps you guarantee related and comprehensive results.

During your searches, first consider the number of results. Only dozens of articles have been published in new areas of research; whereas, hundreds or more articles have been published in a well-established field. In general, the ideal number of results does not exceed 100 to 150 articles per search, because it will not be easy to work through larger numbers, which may show that your search failed to focus closely enough on particular aspects of your topic. Second, briefly review each article. Instead of only reading the article title, you should read the abstract to know the main idea of the article, which can help you shortlist the likely relevant articles. You will have to fully read all articles on your shortlist, to decide if they can be used or not, but you will have a smaller number to read in full. Third, when reading through the articles, be aware of the balance between research and review articles, and recent and older research. According to the nature of the topic, you may keep a different balance. Last but not least, to get more information on evaluating sources, you may consult the Evaluating Books, Journals, Journal Articles and Websites guide.

After your searches, think of your results as a whole. If you are familiar with the topic, you can see if your results represent well-noted researchers or research. If not, why not? Make sure if the results include what you would have expected to find, or if some elements are overlooked.

Step 6: Making the Most of Your Search Results

The purpose of databases is to yield information, so maximize the usefulness of them and gain as much information as possible from your search results.

Whenever you have found a related citation, read the entire record to ensure whether other listed terms might be of use for searching. According to the database you are using, they may be referred to as subject headings, descriptors, concepts, codes, etc.

Check the reference lists of relevant articles for other relevant citations.

If you have come across important researcher(s), conduct an Author search on their name(s).

For the Scopus database, use the cited links to know how other authors have utilized a specific article. For Web of Science, use the Times-cited links.

If a specific search has produced satisfactory results, you may set an alert for it, which commands the database to run an automatic search, and let you know when your area of interest has new articles published.

Step 7: Search Again

It is not enough to do just one search. You will need separate searches for each aspect of your topic. You will also need to conduct your searches again in multiple databases. As you do more searches and read the literature related to your topic, you will find that you need to add to your searches other keywords you come across, or other aspects of the topic you need to study.

6.2   Grey Literature and Retrieval

Systematic reviews aid the analysis and dissemination of evidence, using rigorous and transparent methods to generate empirically attained answers to focused research questions.

Identifying all evidence relevant to the research questions is an essential component, and a challenge, of systematic reviews. Grey literature, or evidence not published in commercial publications, can make important contributions to a systematic review.

Grey literature can provide data not found within commercially published literature, providing an important forum for disseminating studies with null or negative results that might not otherwise be disseminated. Grey literature may thus reduce publication bias, increase reviews' comprehensiveness and timeliness and foster a balanced picture of available evidence.

Grey literature's diverse formats and audiences can present a significant challenge in a systematic search for evidence. However, the benefits of including grey literature may far outweigh the cost in time and resources needed to search for it, and it needs to be included in a systematic review or review of evidence. A carefully thought-out grey literature search strategy may be an invaluable component of a systematic review.

However, the quality of grey literature may vary a lot because it usually does not receive a peer review. The insecurity of grey literature lies in that some organizations may have their own political or social purposes when publishing reports and working papers. In several infamous cases, organizations promoted bogus research for public relations agendas. So you must cross-check information from grey literature against information from other sources. Most grey literature is free of charge. But some sources of grey literature, like market research firms, charge for access to their material.

6.2.1 Typical Grey Literature

Grey literature includes research which is either unpublished or has been published in non-commercial forms, such as reports, policy literature, working papers, theses and dissertations, conference proceedings, newsletters, government documents, speeches, white papers, surveys, fact sheets, etc. Grey literature is usually provided by organizations "on the ground", like government and inter-governmental agencies, non-governmental organizations, and industry to store information and report on activities. It is designed for their use or wider sharing and distribution. Grey literature can be more current than literature in academic journals because it can avoid being delayed or restricted by commercial and scholarly publishing.

1. Document Types in Grey Literature

Grey literature can be best represented by the type of document it contains. The following list of document types can be used to distinguish grey literature.

A: Abstracts, Advertorials, Announcements, Annuals, Article;

B: Bibliographies, Blogs, Booklets, Brochures, Bulletin Boards, Bulletins;

C: Call for Papers, Case Studies, Catalogs, Chronicles, Clinical Trials: Source Document, Codebooks, Conference Papers, Conference Posters, Conference Proceedings, Country Profiles, Course Materials;

D: Databases, Data Papers, Datasets, Datasheets, Deposited Papers, Directories, Discussion Papers, Dissertations, Doctoral Theses;

E: E-prints, E-texts, Enhanced Publications, Essays, ETD (Electronic Theses and Dissertations), Exchange Agreements;

F: Fact Sheets, Feasibility Studies, Flyers, Folders, Forum;

G: Glossaries, Government Documents, Green Papers, Guidebooks;

H: Handbooks, House Journals;

I: Image Directories, Inaugural Lectures, Indexes, Interactive Posters, Internet Reviews, Interviews;

J: Journals, Grey Journals, In-house Journals, Non-commercial Journals, Synopsis Journals;

K: K-blogs;

L: Leaflets, Lectures, Legal Documents, Legislation, Lib Guides;

M: Manuals, Memoranda;

N: Newsgroups, Newsletters, Notebooks;

O: Off-prints, Orations;

P: Pamphlets, Papers (Call for Papers, Conference Papers, Deposited Papers, Discussion Papers, Green Papers, White Papers, Working Papers), Patents, Policy Documents, Policy Statements, Posters, Précis Articles, Preprints, Press Releases, Proceedings, Product Data, Programs, Project [Deliverables, Information Document (PID), Proposals, Work Packages, Work Programs];

Q: Questionnaires;

R: Readers, Registers (Annual Reports, Bank Reports, Business Reports, Committee Reports, Compliance Reports, Country Reports, Draft Reports, Feasibility Reports, Government Reports, Intelligence Reports, Internal Reports, Official Reports, Policy Reports, Progress Reports, Regulatory Reports, Site Reports, Stockbroker Reports, Technical Reports), Reprints, Research Memoranda, Research Notes, Research Proposals, Research Registers, Research Reports, Reviews, Risk Analyses;

S: Satellite Data, Scientific Protocols, Scientific Visualizations, Show Cards, Software, Specifications, Speeches, Standards, State of the Art, Statistical Surveys, Statistics, Supplements, Survey Results, Syllabus;

T: Technical Documentation, Technical Notes, Tenders, Theses, Timelines, Trade Directories, Translations, Treatises, Tutorials;

W: Website Reviews, Web Pages, Websites, White Books, White Papers, Working Documents, Working Papers;

Y: Yearbooks.

2. Conference Papers/Proceedings

Conference papers are papers presented at an academic conference and published as a book or as a special issue of a journal. These can be some hardest forms of grey literature to find. You can readily locate them in library catalogs, or on conference websites. Additionally, you can also limit your search to conference papers with the option in many databases, such as Scopus and Web of Science.

It is much harder to find unpublished conference papers, or conference proceedings yet to be published in the form of printed proceedings. Nevertheless, many databases contain details and occasionally the full-text or sequencing information for papers from academic conferences.

6.2.2 Strategies for Grey Literature Retrieval

1. Where to Search for Grey Literature

To locate grey literature, you need to first find governments and organizations that may publish this kind of information on topics that you care about. And then you may search their websites and pay special attention to website sections, such as "Documents", "Reports", and "Library". Based on the research you have conducted, think about government agencies, non-profits, professional associations, research institutes, and other organizations.

2. Using Bing to Search for Grey Literature

You can merely search a government or institution's site or top-level domain using Bing's site limits. If you intend to find grey literature, it is an efficient way to pair this technique with keywords in Bing.

Bing Custom Searches: Enter your search terms into these pre-built searches to restrict results to particular organization types. Use Search tips for Bing and Bing Scholar to develop your search strings.

Bing Scholar: Bing Scholar contains certain grey literature, mainly theses and dissertations in institutional repositories. You should access Bing Scholar via the Library's website where you can find the "Where can I get this?" links which may lead you to the full text.

3. Search Tips for Bing, Bing Scholar and Other Search Engines

The more search terms are entered, the more specific and concentrated results will be yielded. You need not use AND to connect your search terms. Therefore, each of these searches will become increasingly focused.

By using quotation marks around a phrase, you can instruct a search engine to locate those exact words, in that exact sequence, such as "Airport security" and "full body scans".

As most search engines have no truncation (*) to give the search engine alternative forms to look for, use OR (all caps) and parentheses, such as (airport OR airports OR airline) (scan OR scanner) (ethics OR morals OR rights OR risk).

Use AROUND (all caps) and specific numbers in parentheses to locate words or phrases within some number of words of each other on a web page, such as "airport security" AROUND (3) body scan.

4. Advanced Techniques

When doing advanced searching, the following techniques are popularly used:

1) Exclude terms. The minus sign instructs the search engine to exclude websites which include these terms; e.g., "Full body scans" –MRI –"CAT scan".

2) Searching within a specific site or domain. Use site: to delimit results from a specific website or top-level domain; e.g., "Airport security" "full body scans" site:gov, "Airport security" "full body scans" site:nytimes.com, "Airport security" "full body scans" (site: nytimes.com OR site: washingtonpost.com). Use the minus sign to exclude this domain; e.g., "Airport security" – site: gov.

3) Search in titles. Use intitle: to tell the search engine to locate those words in the titles of results (MUCH more particular results): e.g., intitle: airport intitle: security "full body" (ethics OR rights). Use allintitle: to tell the search engine to locate all the listed words in the titles of results (VERY particular results): e.g., allintitle: airport security "full body".

4) Search for types of files. Use filetype: to tell the search engine to find only certain filetypes; e.g., filetype: pdf, filetype: ppt.

5) Combining advanced search techniques. Use it all together: e.g., intitle: security (intitle: airport OR intitle: airline OR intitle: "air travel") "full body" (scan OR search) (ethics OR moral OR rights OR risk) site: gov, intitle: security (airport OR airline OR "air travel") "full body" (scan OR search) (ethics OR moral OR rights OR risk) (filetype: pdf OR filetype: ppt) site: eu, (airport OR airline OR "air travel") (scan OR scanning OR search OR security) (ethics OR moral OR rights OR risk).

Review Questions

1. What are the typical academic research databases used in scientific research?

2. How can a researcher use academic research databases for scientific research?

3. What is grey literature?

4. How can a researcher search for grey literature for scientific research?

7
Chapter

In-text Citation and Referencing System

Chapter Lead-in: A referencing system is a system used to note information about resources used to construct an academic work. An in-text citation is a reference made within the body of the text of an academic paper. An in-text citation will be used when you refer to, summarize, paraphrase, or quote from another source. For every in-text citation in your paper, there must be a corresponding entry in your reference list. There is no universally adopted referencing system for academic writing. Particular referencing styles are preferred by particular academic disciplines because they work better with the kinds of texts that are most commonly used in that discipline.

7.1 In-text Citation and Reference List

Referencing all your reading in your work demonstrates that you have conducted a thorough and appropriate literature search. Accurate referencing is commensurate with good academic practice and enhances the presentation of your work. It shows that your writing is based on knowledge and informed by appropriate academic reading. You will need to use a referencing style to accurately acknowledge other people's work and ideas.

There are two parts of referencing: citing and creating a reference list. By using the correct style, you will ensure that anyone reading your work can trace the sources you have used in the development of your work, and give you credit for your research efforts and quality. If you do not acknowledge another writer's work or ideas, you could be accused of plagiarism.

7.1.1 In-text Citation

An in-text citation is a reference made within the body of the text of an academic essay. An in-text citation will be used when you refer to, summarize, paraphrase, or quote from another source. For every in-text citation in your paper, there must be a corresponding entry in your reference list. The in-text citation alerts the reader to a source that has informed your writing. The exact format of an in-text citation will depend on the style you need to use. In most cases only the author's last name, date of publication and page number from which the quotation or paraphrase is taken need to be included, with the complete reference appearing in your bibliography (or works cited) page at the end of your essay. The in-text citation should be presented in brackets directly after the text you have quoted or paraphrased so it's easy for the reader to identify. In some cases, in-text citations are presented as a superscript number, with the corresponding number listed in your bibliography.

1. Formats of In-text Citations

The specific format of an in-text citation relies on the style you need to use, for instance, APA. Usually, you only need to include the author's last name, date of publication and page number from which the quotation or paraphrase is taken. At the end of your essay, you can include the complete reference in your bibliography (or works cited) page.

To make the in-text citation easy for the reader to identify, you should present it in brackets immediately after the information you have cited or rephrased. Sometimes, you can also present an in-text citation as a superscript number, and list the corresponding number in your bibliography.

According to APA format, in-text citations may be placed after a direct quote or rephrased text. Remember the in-text citation should right follow direct quotes. If a book is cited, the in-text citation will usually contain the author's surname, the year of publication and the relevant page number or numbers, presented in parentheses. However, if the author is referred to within the text, you do not need to contain it in the in-text citation. If paraphrased information is referred to, a page number is not necessarily required. It relies on if you intend to guide your reader to a particular section. At the end of the paper, remember to add regular citations for the sources to your bibliography.

Be aware that various formats conform to different rules for in-text citations. For instance, MLA format in-text citations usually exclude a publication date and typically contain the author's last name or the first item included in the full citation if not the author's name. In-text citations, according to MLA format, can be presented either in prose or as a parenthetical citation or a combination of the two. Any information about the source already included in the prose, needs not be repeated in the parenthetical citation. Chicago-style in-text citations can follow the (author, date, page number) in-text citation system, like the APA format. Instead, some scholars following the Chicago style prefer to apply a notes and bibliography system, which includes numbered footnotes or endnotes rather than in-text citations. You'll also see different in-text citations within each format, relying on factors such as the type of source and the number of authors.

2. Do's and Don'ts of In-text Citations

DO keep consistent. It is essential to choose a citation style and stick with it in your entire paper. Before starting to write your paper, make sure of the rules for in-text citations, whether you will apply APA format or a different style. Remember to conform to the rules through.

DON'T assume. When citing information from another source, never leave out in-text references, because you think the reader knows where this came from. It is vital to keep a good attitude by being clear about where your research information has been derived from. Otherwise, you may probably face the risk of being accused of plagiarism or being given a poor grade on your assignment.

DO your in-text citations early on. When writing your paper, after you've referenced a work, you should immediately put it down, which can help avoid leaving out any in-text citations. However, if you wait until the very end, you may get stuck in last-minute paper stress. Moreover, in-text citations can provide a list of outside sources you have used in your paper, so writing them early can contribute to the references for your bibliography.

DON'T overuse. If a whole paragraph or a group of sentences refers to information from the same source, you may only need a single in-text citation at the beginning or end of the paragraph. In other words, you do not have to use an individual in-text citation following every directly quoted sentence, which might be a popular misconception.

DO double check. Always check your in-text citations after finishing your paper and before submitting it to your instructor. It is particularly significant if your in-text citations are created during the entire process of paper writing because you can hardly remember the mistake you made two weeks ago. Thus, review your in-text references one last time before handing your paper in.

7.1.2 Reference and Bibliography

Referencing is a conventional practice for acknowledging information sources in academic writing. In other words, by referencing, you make an acknowledgment that you have used the ideas and written material belonging to other authors in your work. Moreover, referencing can show your readers that you have done a literature search appropriately and thoroughly. When creating the reference list, two terms need to be classified: reference and bibliography.

1. Reference

References contain sources that you have directly quoted in your paper. In the body of your paper, you will have at least one corresponding in-text citation for every source. There are different citation styles, such as APA citations, AMA citations, MLA citations, etc.

With references, you can give credit to or mention the name of someone or something, or indirectly convey gratitude towards the sources from where the information is gained. In research methodology, it indicates the items that you have reviewed and referred to in your research work.

When using references, make sure that you only turn to reliable sources, because they can bring more credence and solidify your arguments. It may include books, research papers, or articles from magazines, journals, newspapers, etc.; interview transcripts; Internet sources like websites, blogs, videos watched, and so on. These are used to tell the reader about the sources of direct quotations, tables, statistics, photos, etc., which are included in the research work.

2. Bibliography

Bibliographies include all the sources that you have used for your paper, directly cited or not. You should include in a bibliography every material you consulted in preparing your paper. Chicago citations and Oxford citations are two citation styles using bibliographies.

The bibliography usually appears at the end of the research report. It contains a list of related books, magazines, journals, websites or other publications which the author has consulted during the research for the topic under study. In other words, it consists of all the references cited in the form of footnotes and other major works which the author has studied.

The bibliography helps the reader get information concerning the literature available on the topic. For better presentation and convenient reading, the bibliography can be classified into two parts, wherein the first part includes the names of books and pamphlets considered, and the other includes the names of newspapers and magazines consulted.

Kinds of bibliographies include:

- Bibliography of works cited. It includes the names of those books whose content has been quoted in the text of the research report.
- Selected bibliography. As indicated by its name, the selected bibliography covers only those works that the author assumes are of major interest to the reader.
- Annotated bibliography. In this type of bibliography, the author gives a brief description of the items covered to guarantee readability and also increase the usefulness of the book.

3. Reference vs. Bibliography

Reference and bibliography can both help in recognizing other's work and guide the readers to locate the sources of information. Moreover, they can both avoid plagiarism and prove that you have conducted extensive research on the subject by gaining information from various sources.

However, they are not the same. The reference indicates the sources, which you have cited in the text in the research paper or assignment. Whereas, the bibliography lists all the sources you have read to develop the idea. And their differences lie in the items that are included in them. References are primarily used to recognize and authenticate the research work, while the bibliography is designed to provide the reader with information on the sources relating to the topic.

Both reference lists and bibliographies are placed at the end of a paper and are normally organized alphabetically. A written work can have both a reference list and a bibliography.

7.2 Styles of Typical Referencing Systems

A reference system is a system used to note information about resources used to construct an academic work. They also show work done to support academic studies as well as provide pointers to other academic works that might be of relevance for future research.

There is no universally adopted referencing system for academic writing. Particular referencing styles are preferred by particular academic disciplines because they work better with the kind of texts that are most commonly used in that discipline. The choice of system is up to you, although publishers and journals usually specify exactly how authors should reference their work. This may be enforced very strictly, with precise prescriptions governing the use of footnotes and the format of citations. Other publishers have a more relaxed policy.

No matter which system you choose, be consistent. In other words, you have to use the same style of citation throughout the entire piece of work. Similarly, the style adopted in the bibliography must mirror that used in the references or notes, for this demonstrates you pay due attention to the presentation of your work, and conscientiously live up to the highest academic standards.

7.2.1 Harvard Style

Harvard style is also called the "author-date" style. According to Harvard style, the in-text citation can be placed in brackets in the body of the text or footnotes, including the author's surname, the date of publication, and the page number if a particular page is referred to. Full details are only presented in the bibliography or reference list.

1. In-text Referencing

The in-text reference should contain the authorship and the year of the work. According to the nature of the sentence/paragraph that is being written, in-text references to sources can be cited as described below:

1) Author's name cited in the text. When referencing an author's entire work in your text, it is enough to present the name with the year of publication of the work. On the other hand, if a specific part of the work is mentioned, in a direct or indirect reference, a page reference should be presented.

2) Author's name not cited directly in the text. When you refer to a work or piece of research without mentioning the author in the text, both the author's name and publication year are presented at the relevant point in the sentence or at the end of the sentence in brackets.

3) More than one author cited in the text. Where reference is made to more than one author in a sentence, and they are referred to directly, they are both cited; e.g., "Smith (1946) and Jones (1948) have both shown..." With two or three authors for a work, they should be noted in the text directly using an "and" or indirectly; e.g., "White and Brown (2004) in their recent research paper found..." or "Recent research (White and Brown, 2004) suggests that..." With two or three authors for a work, they should all be listed (in the sequence in which their names appear in the original publication), with the name listed last following an "and". With four or more authors, only the first author should be presented, followed by et al., meaning "and others"; e.g., "Green et al. (1995) found that the majority..." or "Recent research (Green et al., 1995) has found that the majority of..."

4) More than one author not cited directly in the text. List these at the relevant point in the sentence or at the end of the sentence, placing the author's name before the date of publication and separated by a semi-colon and within brackets. Where several publications from a number of authors are referred to, the references should be cited in a chronological order (i.e., earliest first); e.g., "Further research in the late forties (Smith, 1946; Jones, 1948) led to major developments..." "Recent research (Collins, 1998; Brown, 2001; Davies, 2008) shows that..."

5) Several works by one author in different years. If more than one publication from an author illustrates the same point and the works are published in different years, then the references should be cited in a chronological order (i.e., earliest first), e.g., "as suggested by Patel (1992, 1994) who found that..." or "research in the nineties (Patel, 1992, 1994) found that..."

6) Several works by one author in the same year. If an author's several works published in the same year are quoted, they should be distinguished by adding a lower-case letter directly, with no space, after the year for each item; e.g., "Earlier research by Dunn (1993a) found that...but later research suggested again by Dunn (1993b) that..." If several works published in the same year are quoted on a single occasion, or an author has made the same point in several publications, they can all be referred to by using lower-case letters (as above); e.g., "Bloggs (1993a, 1993b) has stated on more than one occasion that..."

7) Chapter authors in edited works. References to the work of an author that appears as a chapter, or part of a larger work that is edited by someone else, should be cited in your text with the name of the author not the editor of the entire work; e.g., "In his work on health information, Smith (1975) states..." In the reference at the end of your paper, details of both the chapter author followed by the details of the whole work should be presented; e.g., "Smith, J., 1975. A source of information. In: W. Jones, ed. 2000. One hundred and one ways to find information about health. Oxford: Oxford University Press. Ch.2".

8) Corporate authors. If the work is by a recognized organization and has no personal author, it is conventionally cited under the body that commissioned the work. This pertains to publications by associations, companies, government departments, etc., like the Department of the Environment or Royal College of Nursing. It is acceptable to use standard abbreviations for these bodies, e.g., "RCN", in your text, with the full name given at the first citing with the abbreviation in brackets; e.g., "...following major pioneering research undertaken by the Royal College of Nursing (RCN) (2018) it has been shown that..." (1st citation) or "...pioneering research in this area (Royal College of Nursing (RCN), 2018) has shown that..." (1st citation); "...more recently the RCN (2018) has shown that..." (2nd citation) or "...the latest research (RCN, 2018) has shown that..." (2nd citation). Be aware that the full name is the preferred format in the reference list. Concerning reports written by specially convened groups or committees, you can cite them by the name of the committee.

9) No author. If the author cannot be identified, use "Anonymous" or "Anon" together with the title of the work (in italics) and date of publication. No effort should be spared to establish the authorship if you wish to apply this work as supporting evidence in an academic submission.

10) For items with no date. The abbreviation "n.d." is used to signify this; e.g., "Smith (n.d.) has written and demonstrated..." "Earlier research (Smith, n.d.) demonstrated that..." No effort should be spared to establish the year of publication if you wish to apply this work as supporting evidence in an academic submission.

11) Finding the year if there are editions or revisions of a book. Remember to use the year of the latest edition of a book, which is usually marked on the back of the title page. The year should be stated in the in-text citation following the author. The number of the edition should be included in your full reference following the title unless it is the first edition. The first-edition books don't show an edition number. Revision is treated as a new edition. The year of the revision should be used as the date. In your full reference add "rev". following the edition number, e.g., "3rd rev. ed."

12) Page numbers. Including the page numbers of a reference can make it easier for readers to trace your sources. This is especially significant for quotations and for paraphrasing specific paragraphs in the texts; e.g., "Lawrence (1966, p.124) states 'we should expect ...'" "This is to be expected (Lawrence, 1966, p.124)..." Pay attention to page numbers: preceded with "p." for a single page and "pp." for a range of pages.

13) Quoting portions of published text. If you intend to cite text from a published work in your essay, the sentence(s) must be presented within quotation marks, and may be introduced by such phrases as "the author states that '...'" or "the author writes that '...'" It is good practice to provide the number of the page where the quotation was found, which can make it easier for a reader to trace the quoted section. You may also indent quotations but should ask your faculty for guidance and the relevant academic regulations.

14) Secondary sources (second-hand references). In the source you are consulting, you may meet a summary of another author's work, which you intend to make reference to in your paper, which is a secondary reference. A direct in-text reference is as: "Research recently carried out in the Greater Manchester area by Brown (1966 cited in Bassett, 1986, p.142) found that..." Here you intend to refer to Brown's work, which you have not read directly. Then you come across the summary of Brown's work from Bassett, who therefore becomes your secondary source. An indirect in-text citation would be: "(Brown, 1966 cited in Bassett, 1986, p.142)". However, you must be aware that Bassett may have propelled Brown's ideas and changed their original meaning. Therefore, if you need to use a secondary reference, you should consult the source instead of depending on someone else's interpretation of a work. As a result, it is recommended not to cite secondary references. At the end of your document, the reference list should only include works that you have read. In the above example you would only list the work by Bassett.

15) Tables and diagrams. If you use selected information from a table or diagram in the text of your essay, it is secondary referencing. If you replicate a whole table or diagram in your essay, you should add a citation below the table to acknowledge where it was found. Finally include the full details of the source.

16) Websites. To quote material from a website, you have to identify its authorship, which might be a named individual or a corporate author, such as an organization, institution or company. If you cannot find a named author, search for a corporate author, which might be in the website name, the "About Us" section or in the URL or web address. Then search around the page for the date of a website, which might be in the headline information or at the bottom of the copyright statement.

2. Reference List

A reference list is designed to make sources easily traced by another reader. Although various publications require different amounts of information, some common elements should be included, like authorship, year of publication and title. The Harvard style sets standards for the order and content of information in the reference. Nevertheless, certain variations of the presentation can be allowed if they are applied consistently. No matter what you are writing, books or journal articles, you must alphabetize all items by author or authorship. For several works from one author or source, you should list them together in a date order, with the earliest work first.

1) Books with one author. For the reference details, you should use the title page rather than the book cover, with the edition included unless it is the first. A first-edition book usually has no edition statement. The following elements are required for a book reference:

Author, Initials., Year. Title of book. Edition. (only include this if not the first edition) Place of publication (this must be a town or city, not a country): Publisher.

The place of publication can commonly be found on the back of the title page at the address of the publishing company.

2) Books with multiple authors. For books with multiple authors, all the names must be included in the order they appear in the document. Use an "and" to connect the last two authors.Certain documents may have many authors, especially in some disciplines. In these cases, it is advisable to seek recommendations from the faculty to make sure whether it is permitted to include only a reduced number instead of all of them. The following elements are required for a reference:

Authors, Initials., *Year. Title of book.* Edition. (only include this if not the first edition) Place of publication: Publisher.

3) Books that are edited. For books which are edited, you should list the editor(s)' surname(s) and initials, followed by "ed." or "eds.". The following elements are required for a reference:

Authors, Initials., ed., Year. *Title of book.* Edition. Place of publication: Publisher.

4) Chapters of edited books. For chapters of edited books, the following elements are required for a reference:

Chapter author(s) surname(s)' and initials., Year of chapter. Title of chapter followed by In: Book editor(s) initials first followed by surnames with ed. or eds. after the last name. Year of book. *Title of book.* Place of publication: Publisher. Chapter number or first and last page numbers followed by full-stop.

5) Multiple works by the same author. For several works by one author and published in the same year, you should differentiate them by adding a lower-case letter after the date, which must be consistent with the citations in the text. For multiple works, the following elements are required for a reference:

Authors, Initials., Year followed by letter. *Title of book.* Place of publication: Publisher.

Works by the same author must be listed in the order referenced in your paper, earliest first as above, which also applies to several authors with the same surname. Alternatively, you may include their initials in the citation. For several works by one author, published in different years, you should arrange them in a chronological order, with the earliest date first.

6) Books—translations/imprints/reprints. For translated works, the details of the translator should be included, and the following elements are suggested for such references:

Authors, Initials., Year. *Title of book.* Translated from (language) by (name of translator, initials first, then surname). Place of publication: Publisher.

For important works of historic significance, you should include the date of the original work together with the date of the translation. For works in another language, you should reference these in the same way as an English language work, with a translation. You are recommended to consult your faculty on the validity of using original language works. For reprints of classic original works, you should include details of the original date of the work and reprinting details, and the following elements are suggested for such references:

Authors, Initials., Original Year. *Title of book.* (Imprint/reprint and then year). Place of publication: Publisher.

7) E-books. For e-books available through a password-protected database from the university library, the following elements are required for a reference:

Authors, Initials., Year. *Title of book.* [e-book] Place of publication: Publisher. Followed by Available through: ARU Library website <https://library.aru.ac.uk> [Accessed date].

For a freely open-access e-book over the Internet like through Google Books, the following elements are required for a reference:

Authors, Initials., Year. *Title of book.* [e-book] Place of publication (if known): Publisher. Followed by Available at: e-book source and web address or URL for the e-book [Accessed date].

For an e-book from particular e-readers and other devices like Kindle, or Nook, the following elements are required for a reference:

Authors, Initials., *Year, Title of book.* [e-book type] Place of publication (if available): Publisher. Followed by Available at: e-book source and web address [Accessed date].

If quoting from an e-book without page numbers, you may use the section heading or chapter heading to locate your quotation, if available.

8) PDF documents. For a PDF version of, for instance, a government publication that is freely available, the following elements are required for a reference:

Authorship, Year. Title of documents. [type of medium] Place of publication (if known): Publisher. Followed by Available at: include web address or URL for the actual pdf, where available [Accessed date].

9) Articles from printed sources—basic journal reference. The following elements are required for a reference:

Authors, Initials., Year. Title of article. *Full Title of Journal,* Volume number (Issue/Part number), Page number(s).

10) Electronic articles. Reference an e-journal article as print if it is available in a print version of the journal. This is often the case where you access an article in pdf format and it uses sequential journal page numbers.

11) Articles from a library database. For articles accessed through a password-protected database from the university library:

Authors, Initials., Year. Title of article. *Full Title of Journal,* [type of medium] Volume number (Issue/Part number), Page numbers if available. Available through: ARU Library website <http://library.aru.ac.uk> [Accessed date].

12) Articles publically available on the Internet. Articles from web-based magazines or journals, including Open Access articles found in institutional repositories:

Authors, Initials., Year. Title of article. *Full Title of Journal or Magazine,* [online] Available at: web address (quote the exact URL for the article) [Accessed date].

13) Articles with DOIs. You can use the DOI (Digital Object Identifier) rather than the format/location/access date:

Authors, Initials., Year. Title of article. *Full Title of Journal,* [e-journal] Volume number (Issue/Part number), Page numbers if available. DOI.

The permanent identifier, DOI, can replace a permanent web address for online articles, which may have the preface http://dx.doi.org/. You may find them at the start/end of an article or on the database landing page for the article. Not every article is assigned a DOI. For the article without a DOI, you can use one of the other e-journal article formats.

14) Journal abstract from a database. For a journal abstract from a database where the full article is inaccessible, the following elements are required for a reference:

Authors, Initials., Year. Title of article. *Full Title of Journal,* [type of medium] Volume number (Issue/Part number), Page numbers if available. Abstract only. Available through: Source [Accessed date].

No effort should be spared to read the full article if you wish to apply this work as supporting evidence in an academic submission.

15) Newspaper articles. For newspaper articles, the following elements are required for a reference:

Authors, Initials., Year. Title of article or column header. *Full Title of Newspaper,* Day and month before page numbers and column lines.

16) Online newspaper articles. For newspaper articles from online newspapers, the following elements are required for a reference:

Author or corporate author, Year. Title of document or page. *Name of newspaper,* [type of medium] additional date information. Available at: <url> [Accessed date].

It is advisable to keep in your files a copy of the first page of any web pages you use.

17) Law reports. It is suggested that you should follow accepted legal citations, which is not part of the Harvard system. For this the following elements are required for a reference:

Name of the parties involved in the law case, Year of reporting (in square brackets where there is no volume, or round brackets as indicated by the reference you are using) abbreviation for the law reporting series, part number/case number/page reference if available.

18) Annual report. The following elements are required for a reference:

Corporate author, Year. *Full title of annual report,* Place of publication: Publisher.

For an e-version of an annual report, the following elements are required for a reference:

Author or corporate author, Year. Title of document or page, [type of medium] Available at: include website address/URL(Uniform Resource Locator)[Accessed date].

It is recommended to keep in your files a copy of the front page of any website you use including reference details.

19) Conference reports and papers. For a conference report, the following elements are required for a reference:

Authorship, Year. Full title of conference report. Location, Date. Place of publication: Publisher.

For a conference paper, the following elements are required for a reference:

Author, Initials., Year. Full title of conference paper. In: followed by editor or name of organization, Full title of conference. Location, Date. Place of publication: Publisher.

20) Reports by organizations. The following elements are required for a reference:

Authorship/Organization, Year. Full title of report. Place: Publisher.

The following elements are required for an e-version:

Authorship/Organization, Year. Full title of report. [type of medium] Place of publication: Publisher. Available at: include web address/URL [Accessed on date].

21) Dissertations and theses. The following elements are required for a reference:

Authors, Initials., Year. *Title of dissertation*. Level. Official name of University.

The following elements are required for an e-version:

Authors, Initials., Year. *Title of dissertation*. Level. Official name of University. Available at <url> [Accessed on date].

22) Course material and lecture notes. You should consult the lecturer to make sure that the lecture notes are in agreement with course material being included in any Reference List. If they are in agreement, and if it is not publicly available, you should give a copy in the Appendix of your work. The citation to the course material in your Reference List should also refer to the Appendix. It is also recommended to trace any sources mentioned in your lecture and read them for yourself. For course material/lecture notes—print version, the following elements are required for a reference:

Lecturer/Author, Initials., Year. Title of item, Module Code Module title. HE Institution, unpublished.

For course material—electronic, the following elements are required for a reference:

Lecturers/Authors, Initials., Year. Title of item, Module Code Module Title [online via internal VLE], HE Institution. Available at: web address if available over the Internet, otherwise indicate if available through Canvas, SharePoint or other virtual learning environment address. [Accessed date]

23) Interviews. You should use a primary source where you have done an interview. You should also check with your faculty office for detailed guidance on what you may include. In addition, you must check with the interviewees to ensure that they will be in agreement with a transcript of the interview. If this will not be publicly available, you should include it as a transcript within an Appendix in your piece of work. In the Appendix you should include details like:

Interviewee's name. Year of interview. Title of interview. Interviewed by …name. [type of medium/format] Location and exact date of interview. Together with the transcript.

24) Reference from a dictionary. When citing a definition from a dictionary, you may use the publisher as the author. The following elements are required for a citation:

(Publisher, Year).

The following elements are suggested for a reference:

Dictionary publisher, Year. *Full title of dictionary.* Place of publication: Publisher.

When using subject-specific or non-generic dictionaries, you may use the author/editor as author, and follow the referencing guidelines for a book.

25) Data sources. When extracting data from a data source, you should acknowledge the source with the year of currency for that data, in an in-text reference. You should include complete details in the reference list.

26) Websites. For websites found on the Internet, the following elements are required for a reference:

Authorship or Source, Year. Title of web document or web page. [type of medium] (date of update if available) Available at: include web address/URL [Accessed date].

If a URL is exceedingly long, you can give the website's home page address with the routing or web path, guiding your reader from the home page to the particular page you have referenced. It is recommended to keep in your files a copy of the first page of any web pages you use.

27) Publications available from websites. For publications found on the Internet, the following elements are required for a reference:

Author or corporate author, Year. Title of document. [type of medium] Place: Producer/ Publisher. Available at: include website address/URL (Uniform Resource Locator) [Accessed date].

It is recommended to keep in your files a copy of the first page of any web pages you use.

28) Blogs. The following elements are required for a reference:

Author, Initials., Year. Title of individual blog entry. *Blog title,* [medium] Blog posting date. Available at: include website address/URL (Uniform Resource Locator) [Accessed date].

29) Social media. The following elements are required for a reference:

Author, Initials., Year. Title of page. [Social Media Type] Day/month post written. Available from:<URL>[Accessed date].

30) Apps. For an app, the following elements are required for a reference:

Authorship, Year. Full text of app article. [mobile app type] Date/month written. Available at:<URL>[Date accessed].

31) DVD, video or film. The following elements are required for a reference:

Full title of DVD or video. Year of release. [type of medium] Director. (if relevant) Country of origin: Film studio or maker. (Other relevant details).

32) Images. When using an image from a book or journal article, you should include an in-text reference and a full reference at the end of the piece of work. Identify the name of the image creator, which may be beneath the image, in the text, or in a list of figures, or copyright statement. If no author or artist is given for the image, you may assume it was made by the author(s) of the book or journal article. For images found on the Internet the following elements are required for a reference:

Author, Year (image created). *Title of work.* [type of medium] Available at: include website address/URL (Uniform Resource Locator) [Accessed date].

If the author is not known, you may begin the reference with the title of the work. If none of these details is known, like author, date, or image title, you should find the file name of the image (for instance by right clicking and checking the properties of the file). If none of the above can be identified, you may start the reference with the subject and title of the work.

7.2.2 Oxford Style

According to Oxford referencing, in-text citations are in footnotes. For the first mention of a text, you should include full details in the footnotes, after which you can use a shortened version. The Footnote/Bibliography method includes two elements: footnotes throughout your assignment, and a bibliography or list of references at the end.

The footnote, as the name shows, is a note (or a reference to a source of information) at the foot (bottom) of a page. In a footnote referencing system, you demonstrate a reference by:

- Putting a small number above the line of the type directly following the source material. The number sits slightly above the line of text and is called a note identifier.
- Putting the same number with a quotation of your source, at the bottom of the page.

Foot noting is numerical and chronological; in other words, the first reference is 1, and the second is 2, and so on. Footnoting makes it easy for readers to find the source of a reference simply by directing their attention to the bottom of the page.

1. Second and Subsequent Footnotes

For second and subsequent references to the same source, you just need the minimum information to clearly show which text is being referred to, instead of providing as many details as for the first note.

In the first footnote, you should give all the necessary information. To refer to the same source again, you may simply provide the author's name, the year of publication and the page number. For instance:

[1] K. Reid, *Higher Education or Education for Hire? Language and Values in Australian Universities,* CQU Press, Rockhampton, 1996, p. 87.

[2] ...

[3] Reid, p. 98.

If in the text you refer to two or more works by the same author, you should include the title:

[1] E. Gaskell, *North and South,* Penguin, Harmondsworth, 1970, p. 228.

[2] E. Gaskell, *The Life of Charlotte Brontë,* Penguin, Harmondsworth, 1975, p. 53.

[3] Gaskell, *North and South,* p. 222.

Subsequent references to articles are done similarly:

[17] M. Doyle, 'Captain Mbaye Diagne', *Granta,* vol. 48, August 1994, pp. 99-103.

[18] ...

[19] Doyle, *Granta,* p. 101.

2. Abbreviations for Subsequent Footnotes

In another way, you can shorten second or subsequent references with Latin abbreviations. For instance:

ibid = same as last entry

You can use "ibid" when two references in a row are from the same source.

op. cit.= as previously cited

You can use "op. cit." when full details of the source have been given in an earlier note. When using "op. cit.", you still need to provide information like the author's name to make the source clear. The abbreviations should be in lowercase, even when they are at the beginning of a note.

For instances:

[11] K. Reid, *Higher Education or Education for Hire? Language and Values in Australian Universities,* CQU Press, Rockhampton, 1996, p. 87.

[12] ibid., p. 26.

[13] M. Doyle, 'Captain Mbaye Diagne', *Granta,* vol. 48, August 1994, p. 99.

[14] Reid, op. cit., p. 147.

3. Citing Different Sources

When citing sources, bibliographical details are important. Bibliographical details refer to information about a source, including the names of the author, the title of the publication, the date of publication, the name of the publisher, the place of publication, URLs and Digital Object Identifiers (DOI). Keep in mind that numbers are given in superscript form in the note.

1) Book. Put the required information in the following order:

author's surname(s) and initial(s), *title of book (underlined or italicized),* publisher, place of publication, year of publication, page number(s).

For instance:

[1] M. Henninger, *Don't Just Surf: Effective Research Strategies for the Net,* UNSW Press, Sydney, 1997, p. 91.

2) Article/Chapter in a book collection. Put the required information in the following order:

author's surname(s) and initial(s), title of article (between single quotation marks), *title of book* (underlined or italicized), editor(s) name, publisher, place of publication, year of publication, page number(s).

For instance:

[2] M. Blaxter, 'Social class and health inequalities', in *Equalities and Inequalities in Health,* C. Carter & J. Peel (eds), Academic Press, London, 1976, pp. 6–7.

3) Journal article. Put the required information in the following order:

author's surname(s) and initial(s), title of article (between single quotation marks), *title of journal or periodical* (underlined or italicized), volume number, issue number, month of publication (if applicable), year of publication, page number(s).

For instance:

[3] M. Doyle, 'Captain Mbaye Diagne'. *Granta*, vol. 48, August 1994, pp. 99–103.

4) Online sources. A website: put the required information in the following order:

author/editor, page title, *website title,* name of sponsor of site (if available), last date site updated, date of viewing, URL.

For instance:

[4] N. Curthoys, 'Future directions for rhetoric—invention and ethos in public critique', in *Australian Humanities Review.* March-April 2001, viewed on 11 April 2001, http://www.lib.latrobe.edu.au/AHR/archive/Issue-April- 2001/curthoys. html.

5) Films, DVDs, and television and radio programs. Put the required information in the following order:

Title, format, publisher, place of recording, date.

For instance:

[5] Strictly Ballroom, DVD, 20th Century Fox, Australia, 1992.

[6] The Nest, television program, SBS Television, Sydney, 15 January 2010.

6) Emails and personal communications. If the details of personal communications should be given in footnotes instead of in the text: give the person's first initial and last name, specify the type of communication, and use the full date. For instance:

[7] P. Gregory, interview with the author, 5 July 2011.

[8] C. Barker, email, 12 January 2012.

4. Bibliography or List of References

Besides full bibliographic information in the footnote or endnote references, you are required to make a separate list of the works you have quoted, because a complete listing of references can provide a clearer idea of your research.

A bibliographic entry includes the same information as a footnote entry, with two major differences, though:

- The author's surname precedes their initial, for sources are alphabetized by author surname.

- Some elements are separated with full stops rather than commas.

An endnote referencing system is also called the Citation-Sequence system. In the text, numbers function as note identifiers. When a source is referred to for the first time, it gets a number. A source keeps the same number in the entire document. In other words, if the source is referred to again, the note identifier is repeated. The notes are collected at the end of the paper, instead of at the bottom of each page. Although footnotes and endnotes serve the same purpose, they are two different systems, so keep consistent and apply one or the other approach.

In long works with multiple sections and/or chapters, it is common to restart numbering at the beginning of each chapter or major section break. With endnotes, this means that your references would be collected in an easily identifiable way for the ease of your reader. If your work is divided into chapters, so is your endnote section.

7.2.3 Vancouver Style

Vancouver referencing is a numeric referencing style, in which every source is allocated a number according to the order that it is arranged in the text. For the same source, referred to again in the text, the same number is retained. The reference list includes a numbered list of quotations with full details. A separate bibliography can also be alphabetized and included, which covers works that you have used for your research but not quoted in the text.

1. Citations

Citing refers to your acknowledging in your text, an idea from a book, journal article, etc., which you have used in your work. You should insert longer-than-two-lines citations as a separate, indented paragraph. In your text, each cited piece of work should be given a unique number, allocated in the order of citation. In your text, you should use the same citation number for the piece of work cited more than once. The number can be put in brackets or written as a superscript. The following are examples of citing different sources.

1) Citing one piece of work; e.g.,

Recent research (1) indicates that the number of duplicate papers being published is increasing.

or

Recent research 1 indicates that the number of duplicate papers being published is increasing.

2) Citing more than one piece of work at the same time: If several pieces of work are cited in the same sentence, the citation number for each piece of work should be included. You can link inclusive numbers with a hyphen, and use a comma to link numbers that are not consecutive. The following example shows how works 6, 7, 8, 9, 13 and 15 have been quoted in the same place in the text; e.g.,

Several studies (6–9, 13, 15) have examined the effect of congestion charging in urban areas.

3) Citing the author's name in your text: The author's name can be cited in your text, but with the inserted citation number; e.g.,

As emphasized by Watkins (2) carers of diabetes sufferers "require perseverance and an understanding of humanity" (p. 1).

4) Citing more than one author's name in your text: For more than one author, use "et al." following the first author; e.g.,

Simons et al. (3) state that the principle of effective stress is "imperfectly known and understood by many practicing engineers" (p. 4).

5) Citing from chapters written by different authors: When quoting from a book which contains chapters written by different authors, you should only cite the author who wrote the chapter rather than the editor of the book.

6) Citing works by the same author written in the same year: When citing a new work written in the same year by the same author as an earlier citation, each work must be given a different number; e.g.,

Communication of science in the media has increasingly come under focus, particularly where reporting of facts and research is inaccurate (4, 5).

7) Citing from works with no obvious author: When citing a piece of work without an obvious author, you should use the so-called "corporate" author. For instance, the author of many online works will be an organization or company instead of individually named authors. In Vancouver style, the author does not need to be included in your citation in your text, but needs to be included in the full reference at the end of your work; e.g.,

The Department of Health (6) advocates a national strategy is creating a framework to drive improvements in dementia services.

or

A national strategy is creating a framework to drive improvements in dementia services (6).

If either a named or corporate author can be identified, "Anon" can be used as the author's name. Be aware: if an author for an online work cannot be found, it is ill-advised to use this work for your research, because you must make sure of the quality and reliability of the information you use and know where the work is from.

8) Citing from multimedia works: When citing a multimedia work, you should commonly use the title of the TV program including online broadcasts or video recordings, or the title of the film as the author. For a video posted on YouTube or other video-streaming web services, you may reference the person who uploaded the video, which might be a username. In Vancouver style, the author does not need to be included in your citation in your text, but needs to be included in the full reference at the end of your work.

9) Citing from an interview or personal communication: You should use the surname of the interviewee/practitioner as the author.

10) Citing a direct quotation: For a direct quote from a book, article, etc. you should use single quotation marks and state the page number; e.g.,

It has been emphasized (2) that carers of diabetes sufferers "require perseverance and an understanding of humanity" (p. 1).

Duplication of charts, diagrams, pictures, etc.; should be dealt with as direct quotes and quoted in the same way as described above.

11) Citing using a secondary reference: When you refer to another author's work and the primary source is not available, a secondary reference appears. When citing such work, you should use both the author of the primary source and the author of the work in which it was quoted, e.g.,

According to Colluzzi and Pappagallo as cited by Holding et al. (7) most patients given opiates do not become addicted to such drugs.

It is recommended that you locate the original work and avoid secondary referencing. If the original work cannot be obtained, you should reference the secondary source, instead of the primary source.

12) Citing an image/illustration/table/diagram/photograph/figure/picture: For any images, illustrations, photographs, diagrams, tables, figures or pictures reproduced in your work, an in-text citation should be provided, together with a full reference as with any other kind of work. You should treat them as direct quotes, by acknowledging the author(s) and showing page numbers; not only in your text where the diagram is referred to, but in the caption you write for it.

2. Reference List

A reference list refers to the list of all the sources you have quoted in the text of your work, including books, journals, etc., listed together in one list, not in separate lists by source type. According to the Vancouver style, the reference list is in numerical order, with every number matching the one in the text. The list is at the end of your work, with books, articles, etc., written in a specific format. The following are some frequently cited references.

1) Journal article: online/electronic:

Author, Title of journal article, *Title of journal* (this should be in italics), Year of publication, Volume number, (Issue number), Page numbers of the article, URL or DOI.

For an online article, you should use its DOI (Digital Object Identifier) in your reference. The DOI is provided by publishers as a permanent identifier to find the article. For the article with a DOI, you do not have to add a date of access. If the article has no DOI, the URL should be used. When reading an article online, check the article details and the DOI can usually be found at the start of the article. If the article is in a full-text database service, like

Factiva or EBSCO, and does not have a DOI or direct URL, then the database URL should be used.

2) Journal article: postprint/in press:

Author(s), Title of journal article, *Title of journal* (this should be in italics), [Postprint/In press], Year of writing, URL [Date of access] or DOI.

A postprint refers to a journal article that has been submitted to the peer review procedure and accepted for publication but is not yet published in a specific journal issue. These articles can be referred to as being "In press". You can figure out what kind of article you have found according to the information provided in the article. DOIs are assigned to articles by journal publishers before publication in a journal issue, so you can use the DOI for postprint/in-press articles, which can guarantee the correct link for the article when it is published in a particular journal issue.

3) Journal article: preprint:

Author(s), Title of journal article, Submitted to/To be published in (if this information is with the article), *Title of journal* (in italics), *Name of repository* (in italics), [Preprint], Year of writing, Version number (if available), URL or DOI (include [Date of access] if there is no version number).

Preprints refer to articles available online before being submitted to the peer review procedure and published in a journal. You may find them in an online repository or on a publisher's website (but not in a particular journal issue). You should make sure which version you are quoting, as preprints are updated at different stages of the publication process. If an article based on the preprint has been published, try to read and quote the published version. Be aware that volume, issue or page numbers are not given to preprint articles.

4) Book: chapter in an edited book:

Author of the chapter, Title of chapter followed by, In: Editor (always put (ed.) after the name), *Title* (this should be in italics), Series title and number (if part of a series), Edition (if not the first edition), Place of publication (if there is more than one place listed, use the first named), Publisher, Year of publication, Page numbers (use "p." before single and multiple page numbers)

5) Book: online/electronic:

Author/Editor (if it is an editor always put (ed.) after the name), *Title* (this should be in italics), Series title and number (if part of series), Edition (if not the first edition), Place of publication (if there is more than one place listed, use the first named), Publisher, Year of publication, URL.

6) Book: print:

Author/Editor (if it is an editor always put (ed.) after the name), *Title* (this should be in italics), Series title and number (if part of a series), Edition (if not the first edition), Place of publication (if there is more than one place listed, use the first named), Publisher, Year of publication.

7) Report:

Author/Editor (if it is an editor always put (ed.) after the name), *Title* (this should be in italics), Organization, Report number: (this should be followed by the actual number in figures), Year of publication.

8) Web page/website:

Author/Editor (use the corporate author if no individual author or editor is named), *Title (this should be in italics)*, URL, [Date of access].

Review Questions

1. What is an in-text citation?
2. What are the formats of in-text citations?
3. What is the referencing system?
4. What are the functions of a reference list?

8 Chapter

Publishing of Scientific Writing

Learning Objectives

After reading this chapter, you should be able to:

1. Know the classification of academic and scholarly journals;
2. Know the process of publishing research in scholarly journals;
3. Know the procedures for presenting and publishing at conferences;
4. Know the process of peer reviewing.

Chapter Lead-in: As a researcher, you make huge strides in advancing essential knowledge. Your achievements can save lives, change the way you understand the world and improve your quality of life. When you're ready to share your knowledge, the best way to do it is by publishing your work. There are different types of academic publishing, such as books and monographs, edited books, book chapters, book reviews, journal articles, conference proceedings, technical reports/scientific reports/white papers, and so forth. Journal articles are the backbone of academic publishing and a wonderful source for research on specific questions. Conference proceedings are most common in the science and engineering fields although in these fields their prominence is declining.

8.1 Publishing Scientific Research in Scholarly Journals

Publication of articles in scholarly journals is one of the most basic activities of scientific research. Submitting scientific research for publishing is a key way for authors to validate their work, and in the wider scheme of things to create novel solutions to complex problems through dialog with fellow researchers. Prospective authors face barriers to publishing their work, including navigating the process of scientific writing and publishing, which can be time-consuming and cumbersome.

8.1.1 Academic and Scholarly Journals

1. Academic Journals

Academic journals refer to periodicals where researchers can have their most recent findings published. From academic journals, researchers and academicians can have access to key information about the leading progress in their field. If there were no academic journals, science is hardly imaginable, because these journals are the first choice for thorough investigation of a scientific issue. Academic journals strictly stick to the peer-review process and conform to the format by publishing mostly the original work. All academic journals observe periodicity or the frequency of release like monthly, bi-monthly, quarterly, half yearly and annual.

Academic journals fall under the academic category, involving all scholarly publications in the fields of engineering, technology, pure and applied sciences, humanity and social sciences. In content, academic journals usually contain articles presenting one's original research as well as reviews of prior works. As typically peer-reviewed journals, academic journals publish theoretical discussions and articles that critically review published work. On the other hand, academic or professional publications which do not undergo peer-review are called professional magazines.

2. Scholarly Journals

Scholarly journals are generally academic journals that encourage academic and scientific research. These journals generally prefer to publish original research works, following a systematic research methodology. The articles published in the scholarly journals are critically evaluated following in-depth analysis of the research data. Scholarly journal articles strictly adhere to a standard format of writing expressing the details about any comprehensible and communicable scientific understanding by fellow researchers.

Once the author accomplishes his task of writing following the standard format and submits the manuscript for publication, it is the responsibility of the scholarly journal to verify whether it is written as per the academic and research norms. Scholarly journals are categorized into multiple subjects like medicine and clinical studies, engineering, biochemistry, etc.

Characteristics of scholarly journals include the following:

- Scholarly articles present the systematic and thorough study of a given topic, usually including original research, experimentation, and surveys.
- Articles are written by a scholar in the field and the author is always identified.
- Authors of scholarly articles always list the sources of their information.
- Articles usually include an advanced vocabulary such as the technical language or jargon, as the reader is supposed to have basic knowledge of the field of study.
- Scholarly journals are also called academic journals or peer-reviewed journals.
- Many scholarly journals are financially supported by professional associations.
- Scholarly journals typically have a serious look, without the advertising, want ads, coupons, and glossy pages found in popular magazines.

3. Academic Journals vs. Scholarly Journals

In many cases, the terms "academic" and "scholarly" can be interchanged, however, EBSCO uses them differently. EBSCO defines academic journals as journals that publish articles with footnotes and bibliographies, and whose target audience is composed of a certain kind of research community. It is a broad classification that contains both "peer-reviewed" journals and journals which are not "peer-reviewed" but targeted for an academic reader. Different from academic journals, scholarly journals are defined as peer-reviewed journals targeted at an academic audience. Although the "peer-reviewed" classification is used at the title level, "article type" information is given for all articles included in a particular issue.

Providing users with "article type" makes them aware that even if a journal may be classified as "peer-reviewed", non-peer-reviewed content like reviews and editorials might be included in the publication, as well.

8.1.2 Publishing Research in Scholarly Journals

Researchers can greatly advance essential knowledge, as their achievements can save lives and improve livelihood. Therefore, as a researcher, you need to have your research published to share your knowledge globally. The first question to ask yourself is, "Do I have a story to tell?" You must have sound conclusions which are based on enough supportive data, because editors and reviewers favor original and innovative research which contributes to their field of study, or exerts immediate impacts. Secondly, ask yourself, "Is there an audience for my research findings?" Make sure your research is interesting enough for a local, regional or worldwide audience. Identifying your audience decides the right journal to hand in your manuscript to.

Several kinds of research articles are listed below:

- Letters and rapid or short communications are designed for quick and early communication of important or original advances, without including too much data or detail.
- Review papers sum up recent developments on a particular topic, without introducing new data.
- Full articles include major data, details, developments and outcomes.
- Research elements enable you to publish research output, like data, software, methods, videos and more, in brief, citable articles.

1. Finding the Right Journal

To reach your intended audience, you must select the right journal for your article. The following strategies and techniques may be used to help find the right journals:

- Consider the kind of article you intend to publish (full-length, letter, review, or research output).
- Check the references in your article, to indicate possible journals of interest.
- Know the journal's aims and scope on its homepage.
- Read the journal's Guide for Authors.
- Make sure the journal is invitation-only; some journals only accept articles after extending an invitation to the author for submission.
- Check the journal's performance for review and publication timelines.
- Check open access options on the journal homepage if you intend to publish your article open access.
- Hand in your paper to just one journal at a time.

Take Elsevier as an instance. The Journal Finder tool (journalfinder.elsevier.com) finds Elsevier journals most closely match your abstracts. An Elsevier journal will be recommended if it has published articles greatly similar to your article. A list of related articles is generated, and the tool can filter according to your preferred standards, like open access options, journal metrics, review time, acceptance rate and production time.

You can choose the best destination for your research or article, using journal metrics alongside information about the journal's scope, editorial board, international outlook and audience. It's recommended to consider more than one metric to help you decide. On the journal homepages, a dedicated Journal Insights section provides information about the journal's:

- Speed—review speed and online publication time;
- Reach—geographic location of corresponding authors and journal usage;
- Impact—impact metrics based on citations received by articles. The average impact of all the articles in a journal is usually used as a proxy for the impact of a particular article, especially when the article has not yet had time to accumulate its citations. It's vital to consider this kind of proxy metric.

2. Submitting and Revising Your Paper

Once your manuscript has been double-checked, it is ready to be submitted to the journal editor via the submission and peer review system. After being submitted, every manuscript is checked for plagiarism, and evaluated carefully to make sure whether it suits the aims and scope of the journal. If journal representatives approve of it, the journal editor will appoint reviewers. Reviewers help determine whether the manuscript is valid, significant and original, by using their checklists to assess the content for scientific value and originality, to make sure the manuscript sticks to both common scientific practice and specific guidelines of the journal, and to ensure that you've referenced properly. After closely looking at the methodology, the validity of the data, and ethical approach, they may recommend changes and improvements to the work. Based on their suggestions, editors will accept, accept with revisions, or reject a manuscript.

3. After Acceptance: Article in Press, Proofing, Share Link and Offprints

After being accepted, articles are published online as an "article in press", and assigned an issue at a later date. You can track your article and citations during this entire process. For the production of a quality article, accurate proofreading and clear marking of corrections are indispensable. When your article has been typeset, an email will be sent to you, with either a PDF attachment of your article or a link to it on the online proofing system. Most academic journals provide authors with a personalized link which gives a duration of free access to the final published version of their article. This link can be used for sharing via email and social networks. Some journals provide offprints; an exact copy of the article published either on paper or as a PDF. You can use the provided Offprint Order Form to order paper offprints before publication. Nevertheless, if your journal does not usually provide paper offprints, you need to pay a small fee.

8.2 Presenting and Publishing at Academic Conferences

8.2.1 Academic Events

Events mostly held in academic environments include seminars, workshops, symposiums, conferences, etc. These events may overlap in the way of their arrangement and participation, so many people cannot tell them apart. Nevertheless, they differ considering the number of delegates, topics covered, duration, etc.

1. Seminar

A seminar refers to a gathering of participants to discuss a delineated topic in interactive sessions. The sessions are often hosted or guided by one or two presenters who see to the discussion being steered in the intended direction. A seminar can have multiple purposes or a single purpose. For example, a seminar may aim for education, such as a lecture, where the participants discuss an academic subject to acquire a better understanding of the subject. Other forms of educational seminars may aim to impart knowledge or skills to the attendees. A seminar can also be inspirational, aiming to motivate the participants to become better people, or to make efforts to apply the skills they have gained from the seminar.

In some cases, seminars are just opportunities for business persons to network and meet other like-minded participants. Such seminars may help the attendees reach the next level in their careers by enabling them to make certain potentially valuable contacts. For instance, a trade seminar gathers a broad cross-section of the community together, including government officials, business persons and the general public. These seminars usually involve workshops and the presentation of white papers and aim to contact various vendors and establish new connections.

2. Workshop

A workshop is an instructional or informative class that mainly teaches specialized skills or explores a specific subject. In short, a workshop is about using a place to build something hands-on. Workshops are usually presented by educators, subject matter experts, managers or other leaders that boast knowledge of a specific subject or mastery of particular skills. The presenters can enhance the effectiveness of their presentations through careful organization and presentation practice. Workshops, according to the topic, may last long or short.

Comparatively speaking, seminars are often more academic and less hands-on than workshops. Seminars are mostly oriented toward educational topics, featuring one or more experts on the subject matter. Whereas, workshops tend to be less formal, requiring more participation from attendees than seminars. Workshops are designed for the attendees to get hands-on experience and acquire new skills with the help of the instructor.

3. Symposium

A symposium provides a formal, academic setting for experts in their fields to participate. It can be compared to a small-scale conference for there are fewer delegates. The experts present their speeches on a delineated topic of discussion, after which there are the usual discussions on the topic. The main feature of a symposium is that it addresses a single topic or subject and experts finish delivering all the lectures within a single day. Besides usual presentations, symposiums may also include sessions that encourage more discussion and exchange of ideas, like panel discussions, with well-known experts in the topic of the symposium being the presenters and panelists.

In comparison with other academic events, a symposium is somehow casual, for the delegates are under less pressure to perform or deliver speeches in the best possible way. There are also cocktail receptions, lunch breaks, speakers dinner, tea, or snacks, but it is a more formal networking occasion instead of a party. Contrary to big annual conferences, symposiums are usually organized when it is needed to conduct in-depth discussion of a given "hot topic" of research, and therefore, the themes may vary from year to year. The presenters and panelists at a symposium already know each other somehow, for they share interest and expertise in the topic of the symposium. Students and trainees usually attend a symposium as audience members to learn from renowned researchers rather than to present their work.

4. Conference

A conference is a formal meeting for attendees to exchange their views on different topics. Conferences are organized in large venues like a congress center, with parallel sessions covering different subtopics of a broad field of research over multiple days. They can be interdisciplinary, inviting attendees from various fields of research with interest in a common topic, and presenters include both renowned researchers and experts, and students and trainees.

A conference can take place between just two people, such as the student and his instructor; a conference can also involve many attendees. But generally speaking, a conference is a meeting of lots of people from different places at the conference venue, who discuss their views on some topics. A conference usually lasts for several days, and according to its agenda, formal discussions take place on chosen days. Conferences can be national or international. National conferences are participated mainly by experts in a specific field from within the country that the conference is held in; whereas international conferences are much bigger, with participants throughout the world.

Large conferences provide a significant annual chance for exchange and networking among academics. For experienced researchers, international conferences are a great venue not only to reunite with friends and collaborators but also to attract potential young researchers to join their group. For students or trainees, having the opportunity to present their research at a yearly conference not only improves their CVs greatly but also gives them a rare chance to meet with future employers and potential collaborators. Evening social events, as a vital part of conferences, provide a more casual atmosphere for attendees to interact and network after the formal meetings of the day.

8.2.2 Presenting and Publishing at Academic Conferences

An academic conference is also called a research conference, academic congress, academic meeting or symposium. It is a gathering for researchers to present their findings and learn about the latest work in their field. Academic conferences are commonly organized by associations or groups of independent researchers, and are usually supervised by a scientific committee that guarantees the academic quality of the research presented at these events.

Academic conferences vary in shape and size, ranging from small local meetings to global events with thousands of international participants. Some conferences focus on highly specialized topics within one single discipline; whereas, other conferences might be interdisciplinary, involving various perspectives from academics, the industry and practitioners across multiple disciplines. It is by all means an intellectually exciting experience for researchers to attend an academic conference, because they can get a chance to look beyond the fence and see what is happening outside of a given specialty. In addition, they can make new contacts, facilitate their research and propel their career. However, many people fail to enjoy all the benefit that an academic conference provides, because they are not sufficiently familiar with academic conferences, which seems like a whole new world, full of abstracts and camera-ready papers, peer review and poster sessions.

1. What May Happen at an Academic Conference

At academic conferences, academics and researchers present and discuss their latest work, and find the latest and interesting developments in their specialty. Almost everyone who attends such a conference also presents at it. Therefore, academic conference often has a program filled with short presentations covering various topics, usually arranged into parallel streams, or in other words, simultaneously running sessions. Nowadays, the rigid, predefined structure of the conventional academic conference format is changing, and more and more conferences in the academic world are trying innovative styles of presentation and interaction. Nonetheless, the typical presentations at an academic conference can be categorized into the following groups.

1) Plenary sessions. All delegates are encouraged to attend a plenary session, which includes a keynote session, panels or other kinds of presentation.

2) Keynote sessions. A keynote session often appeals to conference delegates, because keynote speakers usually set the tone for the entire conference and enhance a sense of collective academic efforts.

3) Panel sessions. Panels are for experts and researchers to exchange views, discuss and debate on a topic. These sessions may take different forms, with panellists making prepared statements or directly answering questions from the session chair or the audience.

4) Oral sessions. These sessions usually involve multiple presenters delivering talks on separate papers with common themes or topics. Each presenter is given approximately 10 minutes to speak with some more time to answer questions from the audience after the presentation.

5) Poster sessions. A typical poster presentation usually displays a physical or digital poster in the halls at an academic conference. Posters are often shown at the same time (usually over several hours) in the same room. Delegates do not have to worry about time constraints, instead, they can take their time studying work and exchanging ideas with the presenter in detail.

6) Workshops. At conferences, tutorials or workshops are often held on subjects, such as science communication or advice on getting published in leading journals. These are usually designed for researchers who are beginning their careers; thus they can enjoy the additional benefit of networking with participants at a similar career level.

2. Reasons to Attend an Academic Conference

You may think the main point of attending an academic meeting is to present your research. Certainly, it is important, for it means presenting your ideas to experts in your specialty and eliciting questions and comments which can improve your work. However, presenting is only one reason to attend an academic conference. By attending conferences, you can catch up with the latest trends in your specialty, because articles handed in to an academic journal will be re-drafted repeatedly and it often takes months for them to be published, while at academic conferences you may learn about rough-hewn but recent findings. By attending presentations, you will gain sufficient information to determine if you intend to find out more about the speaker's work, for a well-structured academic conference provides you with plenty of information.

One of the most important reasons for attending an academic conference lies in meeting other researchers. Conferences provide participants with great chances to have conversations with the speakers whose presentations caught their attention, either by approaching the presenters in the hall or hitting them up on the conference app to arrange a meeting over a cup of coffee.

By attending social events at conferences, you can hear others' perspectives on careers and research. For example, mealtimes are a valuable chance to talk about work in a relaxed manner or discuss the presentations that have impressed you the most. Especially as young researchers, you should take advantage of those occasions designed for event first-timers, to find your tribe. By attending a conference, you'll get a set of proceedings, which is the official record of a conference, either a hard copy or a digital version. In them, you may find an abstract, and sometimes the full paper of each presentation from the conference. With this treasure of the latest research in your field, you can introduce yourself to speakers you did not get the chance to meet in person for further exploration and research.

3. Submitting to a Conference

If you want to have your work accepted for publication at a conference in your specialty, you should first check a call for papers (also known as a call for abstracts or conference announcement email) on conference announcement sites. From the call for papers, you can learn about conference topics and submission details.

Secondly, you have to decide what kind of presentation to submit your work for, a talk (as part of an oral session) or a poster. Certainly, a talk can get your name out there, for it might be part of a large oral session. However, if your work is not ready for a talk yet, you may submit a poster. You should present your poster in an effective way, which alone can convey the main points of your work, and you are there to answer any extra questions without a time limit. Scientist Sees Squirrel gives a complete breakdown of the oral vs poster pros and cons.

Thirdly, follow the conference submission guidelines precisely. Submissions can take the form of an abstract, an extended abstract or a paper. A conference abstract is designed to sum up in a single paragraph, the main aspects of your paper, and it is usually the only part of your paper that conference organizers will read. Therefore, learning to write a strong, complete and concise abstract for your submission is a skill that will serve you well throughout your career.

Finally, make corrections as requested. Before being accepted by an academic conference, submissions are evaluated by a panel of reviewers, including experts in their field who give written, unbiased feedback on submissions. To keep the impartiality of the review process, your submission may be reviewed under single-blind conditions (the reviewer knows who the researcher is) or double-blind conditions (the reviewer does not know who the researcher is). Reviewers may request corrections if they think it's necessary. The corrected copies of submissions are finally ready to be published as part of the conference proceedings.

4. Funding Your Trip

The costs of attending an academic conference may add up, including registration fees, airfares and accommodation. Conference organizers may commonly offer cheaper fees to researchers from developing countries or beginners in their careers. Some universities or research institutes may also help cover the cost of fees because they require you to publish at conferences. In addition, travel grants can be applied by researchers who have just begun their careers. You may consult your academic supervisor, your department head or your HR department about what options of funding there are for you. You may also ask the conference organizers directly if there is little information on the conference website. Additionally, conferences also look for student volunteers on site and you may get a volunteering role, for which you do not need to pay full fees. It's also worth following the conferences' social media hashtags or searching on its mobile app to know whether any delegates who live near the venue want to host people in their homes. Or if anyone intends to split the cost of accommodation.

8.3 Peer Reviewing for Academic and Scientific Publishing

8.3.1　Peer Review: What and Why

1. What Is Peer Review?

Peer review refers to the process of having an author's academic work or research scrutinized by other experts in the same field. Peer review is designed to fulfill two major purposes. Firstly, it determines the validity, significance and authenticity of the work and makes sure that only high-quality study is published, particularly in prestigious journals. Secondly, peer review also aims to enhance the quality of articles that are regarded as proper for publication, by suggesting that authors improve the quality of their work, and correct all errors before publication.

The Philosophical Transactions of the Royal Society is considered the first journal to formalize the peer review process under the editorship of Henry Oldenburg (1618–1677). Ever since then, peer review has remained a formal part of scientific communication. Despite many criticisms about the integrity of peer review, the majority of the research community still sees peer review as the best widely accepted method of scientific evaluation and research validation. Moreover, according to a survey by the Publishing Research Consortium in 2015, 82 percent of researchers agree that peer review plays a pivotal role in scientific communication and academic publishing.

2. Impact of Peer Review

Peer review serves as the foundation of the academic publication system because it effectively has an author's work scrutinized by other experts in the field. In this way, authors will strive to make high-quality research that will advance the field in turn. Peer review also helps maintain honesty and originality in the development of science. Unless a scientific hypothesis or statement has been published in a peer-reviewed journal, it is usually not accepted by the academic community. The Institute for Scientific Information (ISI) only deems peer-reviewed journals as candidates to get Impact Factors. Peer review has been a well-established formal part of scientific communication for around 350 years.

3. Benefits of Peer Review for Students

Peer review gets students engaged with writing and helps them understand the link between their writing and their coursework in ways that undergraduates often overlook. It encourages students to cultivate self-reflexivity which hones critical thinking skills. In this way, students may become lifelong thinkers and writers who know how to question their work, values, and engagement rather than just responding to a prompt. Through peer review, the writing process becomes more collaborative, which offers students chances to learn from each other. Many students report that they learn as much or more from finding and articulating weaknesses in a peer's paper as from incorporating peers' feedback into their work.

Peer review can force students to clarify the goals of the assignment because they have to focus on goals when determining if individual student examples meet the requirements. In this way, they can avoid being distracted by grammar and mechanics or by their anxiety. Peer review offers students contemporary models of disciplinary writing. Students are taught writing skills in English class in high school, therefore, their models for good writing may be too general to meet the requirement of their specialty. Peer review gives them a communal space to learn about writing in the disciplines.

Peer review allows students to formulate their ideas as they articulate them to classmates and as they raise questions about their classmates' writing, which improves writers at all skill levels, in all classes, and at all stages of the writing process. Students can gain professional experience from peer review because peer review is a skill with practical application. In other words, professionals in the field publish by the process of peer review, and managers and co-workers provide feedback in the workplace by the process, too. Last but not least, peer review can avoid common lower-level writing errors and minimize errors in the last-minute drafting.

8.3.2　Peer Review: Types and Process

1. Types of Peer Review

There are different types of peer review, so you have to know the respective rules by checking which variant is used by the journal that you are working on. Usually, one type of review is preferred by a subject community. However, if you are uncertain about the peer review model employed by the journal, consult the journal's home page or directly contact the editorial office.

1) Single anonymized review. This type of review hides the identities of the reviewers from the author because reviewer anonymity contributes to impartiality of decisions. It is the traditional model of reviewing and is the most common type till now.

2) Double anonymized review. This type of review keeps both the reviewer and the author anonymous. This method has some advantages. Firstly, author anonymity avoids reviewer bias, based on an author's sex, nationality, academic status or prior publication history, etc. Secondly, papers written by well-established authors are judged by the content of their articles, instead of their reputation.

3) Triple anonymized review. This type of review not only keeps reviewers anonymous but hides the author's name from both the reviewers and the editor. Articles are kept anonymous when submitted and are handled in such a way as to possibly avoid potential bias towards the author(s).

4) Open review. This type of review lets both the reviewer and the author known to each other during the peer review process, aiming at greater transparency during and after the peer review process. Open peer reviews consist of:

- publication of reviewers' names on the article page;
- publication of peer review reports alongside the article, signed or anonymous;
- publication of peer review reports (signed or anonymous) together with authors' and editors' responses alongside the article;
- publication of the paper after a quick check and opening a discussion forum to the community who can comment, named or anonymous.

Many people maintain that this method can effectively minimize malicious comments, prevent plagiarism, stop reviewers from following their agenda, and encourage open, honest reviewing. Whereas, others deem open review a less honest process, because politeness or fear of retribution may cause a reviewer to withhold or understate criticism.

5) More transparent peer review. Generally speaking, transparency is the foundation of trust in peer review. Therefore, many journals release the name of the article's handling editor on the published paper. Some journals also give details about the number of reviewers who reviewed the article before acceptance. Moreover, most journals let reviewers know about the editor's decision and their peers' recommendations to give updates and feedback to reviewers.

2. Peer Review Process

After a researcher finishes a study and writes a paper, describing the purpose, experimental methods, results, and conclusions of the research, his or her manuscript is handed in to a journal in a relevant field, which is called pre-submission. The editors of the journal will review the paper to check whether the subject matter corresponds with that of the journal and whether it fits with the editorial platform. Very few manuscripts pass this initial assessment. If the journal editors believe the paper meets these requirements and is from a reliable source, they will send it to renowned researchers in the field for a formal peer review. Editors will monitor the peer review process, by making sure that peer reviews are conducted impartially, effectively and timely and that no conflicts of interest are involved in the peer review process.

When reviewers get a paper, they put it under scrutiny to assess the validity of the science, the quality of the experimental design, and the appropriateness of the methods used. Reviewers also evaluate the significance of the findings, determine the originality of the research, and make sure the work will advance the field. In addition, reviewers find scientific errors and references, missing or incorrect. The editor will get recommendations from peer reviewers, regarding if the paper should be accepted, rejected, or revised before publication in the journal. The editor will mediate author-reviewer discussion to identify the priority of some review requests, recommend areas to be strengthened, and overrule recommendations beyond the study's scope. If the paper is accepted, as per suggestion by the peer reviewer, the paper enters the production stage, and the editors will slightly adjust and format it, before it is finally published in the scholarly journal.

3. Who Conducts Reviews?

Peer reviewers can be anyone with competence and expertise in the subject areas of the journal, including scientific experts with specialized knowledge of the content of the manuscript, and scientists with a more general knowledge base. Reviewers can range from young and up-and-coming researchers to old masters in the field. According to a study on peer review by the Publishing Research Consortium, a reviewer on average, conducts around eight reviews on the yearly basis. Journals often have a pool of reviewers with different backgrounds for various perspectives, and they also keep a big reviewer bank, to prevent reviewers from getting overwhelmed or exhausted from reviewing several manuscripts at the same time.

Review Questions

1. What are academic and scholarly journals?
2. What is the process of publishing research in scholarly journals?
3. What is the process of presenting and publishing research articles at academic conferences?
4. What is the process of peer reviewing?

9
Chapter

Ethical Issues in Scientific Writing

Learning Objectives

After reading this chapter, you should be able to:

1. Know the principles of research ethics;

2. Know typical scientific misconducts (plagiarism, text recycling);

3. Know the types of errors in scientific writing and the way to fix errors.

Chapter Lead-in: Ethics are broadly the set of rules, written and unwritten, that govern the expectations of your own and others' behavior. Effectively, they set out how you expect others to behave and why. While there is a broad agreement on some ethical values, there is also wide variation on how exactly these values should be interpreted in practice. The ethics of scientific research are somewhat unique within professional ethics in the sense that good science requires the ethical practice of science. Research ethics are the set of ethics that govern how scientific and other research is performed at research institutions such as universities, and how it is disseminated.

9.1 Ethics and Misconduct in Scientific Writing

9.1.1 Research Ethics: Significance and Principles

Research ethics is a field of ethics that works to apply moral principles to scientific pursuits, particularly research. Many different ethical issues come up in the course of scientific advancement. In general, the field of ethics is typically concerned with what is right and what is wrong in a very broad sense. In research, ethics are primarily concerned with what is acceptable and what is unacceptable. It is important to adhere to ethical norms in research.

Although codes, policies and principles are very important and useful, like any set of rules, they do not cover every situation, they often conflict, and they require considerable interpretation. It is therefore important for researchers to learn how to interpret, assess and apply various research rules and how to make decisions and act ethically in various situations.

Research ethics apply moral principles to scientific pursuits, especially research. In the course of scientific advancement, many ethical issues may pop up, like animal testing and research and development of weapons. Generally speaking, ethics tell what is right apart from what is wrong in a rather broad sense. In research, ethics distinguish between what is acceptable and what is unacceptable. In most cases, issues in research ethics are concerned with moral issues, but there might be exceptions, particularly involving the extreme subjectivity of ethics and morals.

Research ethics are particularly important to medical researchers because they need to conduct much testing and trial work before they can put some medical research into practice. Before releasing some medication to the market, it can probably save lots of time, if dangerous drugs can be tested on humans. Nevertheless, it is unethical to do so. On the other hand, animal testing is another concern in research ethics in the medical area because many people reckon it unethical to test drugs and procedures on animals as well.

Another issue of research ethics is whether research data in publications present the original ones truthfully and accurately. It is severely unethical to publish false data, for it misguides future researchers as they gain understanding from false ideas. It is also unethical not to report unfavorable results; as failed experiments may contribute to science as well. Therefore, it is extraordinarily important to submit an accurate and complete research. If any human errors happen during the research, it is vital to present them as well when the results are published.

Research ethics also influence what topics should and should not be studied, although this is a much more subjective area involving politics and religion. For example, many people consider weapons research as unethical because the product of such research will threaten lives. Others regard embryonic stem cell research to be a main ethical issue because to them the embryos used are human lives that are extinguished for the research. Many people believe the most important goal is adding to the body of human knowledge; hence science should not be affected by religious, political, or even ethical issues.

1. Significance of Ethical Norms in Research

The following reasons explain why it is significant to abide by ethical norms in research. First, standards promote the aims of research, including knowledge, truth, and avoidance of error. For instance, prohibitions against falsifying, fabricating or misinterpreting research data uphold the truth and minimize error.

Second, ethical norms promote the values that are essential to collaborative work, including trust, accountability, mutual respect and fairness because research usually involves lots of cooperation and coordination among different people in different disciplines and institutions. For instance, many ethical standards in research are intended to protect intellectual property rights and encourage collaboration, like guidelines for authorship, copyright and patenting policies, data sharing policies, and confidentiality rules in peer review.

Third, many ethical norms help guarantee that researchers can be held accountable to the public. For instance, policies on research misconduct, conflicts of interest, human subjects protections, and animal care and use are necessary to ensure that researchers funded by public money can shoulder responsibility to the public.

Fourth, ethical norms in research also help get public support for research, as people tend to fund a research project if they can trust the quality and integrity of the research.

Finally, many norms of research uphold various other important moral and social values, including social responsibility, human rights, animal welfare, compliance with the law, and public health and safety. Ethical negligence in research can do severe harm to human and animal subjects, students, and the public. For instance, a researcher who makes up data in a clinical trial may harm or even kill patients, and a researcher who fails to adhere to regulations regarding radiation or biological safety may endanger his or her health and safety or the health and safety of staff and students.

2. Principles for Research Ethics

Because ethics are crucial for the conduct of research, it is not surprising that various professional associations and universities have employed particular codes, rules, and policies concerning research ethics. Many government agencies also have ethics regulations for funded researchers. The following roughly summarizes certain ethical rules that different codes address:

1) **Honesty:** Strive for honesty in all scientific communications. Present data, results, methods and procedures, and publication status with honesty. Do not fabricate, falsify, or misrepresent data. Do not deceive colleagues, research sponsors, or the public.

2) **Objectivity:** Strive to avoid bias in experimental design, data analysis, data interpretation, peer review, personnel decisions, grant writing, expert testimony, and other aspects of research in which objectivity is expected or required. Avoid or minimize bias or self-deception. Report personal or financial interests that may influence research.

3) **Integrity:** Keep your promises and agreements; act sincerely; keep consistent in thought and action.

4) **Carefulness:** Avoid careless errors and negligence; examine your work and the work of your peers carefully and critically. Keep good records of research activities, including data collection, research design, and correspondence with agencies or journals.

5) **Openness:** Share data, results, ideas, tools and resources. Be open to criticism and new ideas.

6) **Transparency:** Report methods, materials, assumptions, analyses, and other information needed to evaluate your research.

7) **Accountability:** Be responsible for your research and be prepared to give an account (an explanation or justification) of your research project and its purpose.

8) **Intellectual property:** Respect patents, copyrights, and other forms of intellectual property. Do not use unpublished data, methods, or results without permission. Properly acknowledge all contributions to your research. Never plagiarize.

9) **Confidentiality:** Protect confidential information, including papers or grants submitted for publication, personnel records, trade or military secrets, and patient records.

10) **Responsible publication:** Publish to advance research and scholarship, not just to promote your career. Avoid unnecessary and duplicative publication.

11) **Responsible mentoring:** Help educate, mentor, and supervise students. Improve their welfare and let them decide on their own.

12) **Respect for colleagues:** Treat your colleagues with respect and fairness.

13) **Social responsibility:** Strive to increase social good and avoid or mitigate social harms through research, public education, and advocacy.

14) **Non-Discrimination:** Never discriminate against colleagues or students based on gender, race, ethnicity, or other factors unrelated to scientific competence and integrity.

15) **Competence:** Keep and improve your professional competence and expertise through lifelong learning. Promote your overall competence in science step by step.

16) **Legality:** Abide by related laws and institutional and governmental policies.

17) **Animal care:** Duly respect and care for animals when using them in research. Do not conduct wasteful or ill-designed experiments on animals.

18) **Human subjects protection:** When researching on human subjects, minimize harms and risks and maximize benefits; honor human dignity, privacy, and autonomy; treat vulnerable populations with precaution; and strive to distribute the benefits and burdens of research with fairness.

9.1.2 Scientific Misconduct: Types and Guidelines

1. Types of Scientific Misconduct

Scientific misconduct refers to a deviation from standards of scientific research, study and publication ethics. Different kinds of scientific misconduct may occur at any stage in a research protocol, from the origination of the research study to the publication of the results. Here are the common kinds of scientific misconducts that peer reviewers and journal editors mind.

1) **Misappropriation of ideas:** Taking the intellectual property of others, maybe as a result of reviewing someone else's article or manuscript, or granting an application and proceeding with the idea as your own.

2) **Plagiarism:** Using someone else's words, published work, research processes, or results without giving proper credit via full citation.

3) **Self-plagiarism:** Recycling or reusing your work without proper disclosure and/or citation.

4) **Impropriety of authorship:** Claiming undeserved authorship on your behalf, excluding material contributors from co-authorship, including non-contributors as authors, or handing in multi-author work to journals without permission of all named authors.

5) **Failure to meet legislative and regulatory requirements:** Willfully disobeying rules regarding the safe use of chemicals, care of human and animal test subjects, improperly using investigative drugs or equipment, and improperly using research funds.

6) **Violation of accepted research practices:** Proposing research study or manipulating experiments to produce preferred results, using deceptive statistical or analytical methods to

produce preferred results, or inappropriately reporting results to present a misleading outcome.

7) Falsification of data: Fabricating the data entirely.

8) Failure to support validation of your research: Refusing to supply complete datasets or research material needed to validate your results through a reproduced study.

9) Failure to respond to known cases of unsuccessful validation attempts: Not retracting published research which is found flawed from the journal that published it.

10) Inappropriate behavior about suspected misconduct: Not cooperating with claims of misconduct made against you, not reporting known or suspected misconduct, destroying evidence related to any claim of misconduct, retaliating against any persons involved in a claim of misconduct, deliberately making false claims of misconduct.

2. Guidelines for Scientific Misconduct

Among various guidelines and rules for the conduct of scientific research, the major set of guidelines is the APA (American Psychological Association) statement on scientific honesty and integrity. According to this statement, the first rule is that a scientist must provide formal written material assuring what he/she is doing when studying a topic, including an account of his or her methods, data and observations. This assurance is referred to as a "VA", or statement of responsibility. Another rule is that a researcher must ensure that his or her conforms to the guidelines of peer review and replication. Another important element is that a Publication Review Statement must be signed by a scientist and every coauthor when a paper is submitted to a journal. And journal editors take this issue rather seriously.

If the validity of a body of work (like the manipulation of images) is questioned, readers or members of the academic community should hand in a formal "expression of concern" about improper behavior having occurred within this research. Then the editor will decide whether the alleged misconduct is based on real evidence. In some countries, this may also be investigated by a research ethics committee or an office of research integrity. Other reasons for an expression of concern from readers might be around the nature of any experiments that were conducted or whether there was solid evidence questioning the ethical behavior of researchers conducting a clinical trial, for instance. There are clear ethical guidelines that apply to published research with human subjects involved.

When a researcher picks a particular sample or source of data from which to study a specific topic, this must be mentioned in the article. If the sample is selected because of lack of quality, it is unethical to use that source. If multiple samples are used, each must have been checked for reliability.

Some guidelines also apply to the reporting of results. Avoid reporting research with missing or incorrect data or with conclusions that do not match the sample. Other unethical behavior includes misrepresenting data, pretending to have a scientific relationship to something, or plagiarizing someone else's work.

All in all, governmental agencies and scientific review boards have regarded ethics as a matter of continuing concern, as they consider it vital for science to be objective, consistent and honest in its work. If reviewers believe that the work is being compromised by certain unethical actions, that can harm the value and integrity of the scientific enterprise. If someone accuses of scientific misconduct, it is crucial to investigate it properly and immediately.

9.2   Plagiarism and Errors in Scientific Writing

9.2.1 Plagiarism: Common Sense

Plagiarism is presenting someone else's work or ideas as your own, with or without their consent, by incorporating it into your work without full acknowledgment. All published and unpublished material, whether in manuscript, printed or electronic form, is covered under this definition. Plagiarism may be intentional, reckless, or unintentional. Under the regulations for examinations, intentional or reckless plagiarism is a disciplinary offense.

However, not all types of plagiarism are alike. When analyzing whether something is an act of plagiarism, the determination of whether it was intentional or unintentional plays an important role. That is why knowledge about plagiarism is a key learning component at colleges and universities. It addresses the gravity of both intentional and unintentional plagiarism.

Nearly all expression of original ideas is deemed intellectual property and falls under copyright protection, like original inventions, as long as it is recorded in a certain way, like a book or a computer file.

The following are examples of plagiarism:

- turning in someone else's work as your own;
- copying words or ideas from someone else without giving credit;
- failing to put a quotation in quotation marks;
- providing incorrect information about the source of a quotation;
- changing words but copying the sentence structure of a source without giving credit;
- making up the majority of your work with copied words or ideas from a source, whether you give credit or not.

Citing sources can help prevent most cases of plagiarism. In other words, to avoid plagiarism, you must acknowledge that some material has been borrowed and give your reader the information necessary to track that source.

1. Plagiarism in Using Images, Videos and Music

It is plagiarism to use an image, video or piece of music in your work without appropriate permission or proper citation. The following activities are very common cases of plagiarism in current society:

- Copying media (images in particular) from other websites to paste them into your own papers or websites.
- Making a video with footage from others' videos or with copyrighted music as part of your soundtrack.
- Performing another person's copyrighted music (i.e., playing a cover).
- Composing a piece of music that borrows a lot from another composition.

In some situations, it is hard to decide if the copyrights of a work are being offended. For instance:

- Using a photograph or scan of a copyrighted image (e.g., using a photograph of a book cover to represent that book on one's website).
- Recording audio or video with copyrighted music or video playing in the background.
- Recreating a visual work in the same medium (e.g., taking a photograph which uses the same composition and subject matter as someone else's photograph).
- Recreating a visual work in a different medium (e.g., making a painting with close resemblance of another person's photograph).
- Remixing or altering copyrighted images, video or audio, even though done so in an original way.

The legality of such situations depends on the intent and context within which they are created. The following two methods are safe to take regarding similar situations: avoid them completely or get the works' usage permissions and cite them appropriately.

2. Consequences of Plagiarism

Plagiarism is wrong because it fails to give credit to the person or entity that produced the work originally. It is a form of academic dishonesty for students and academics. But this does not mean you cannot use others' work, because it is an important part of academic writing to draw upon present ideas and research. However, you must tell your words and ideas apart from those of others, which gives due credit to the works you used and enables your audience to find sources of your ideas and verify the evidence on their own. The consequences of plagiarism may range from failing an assignment to severe legal implications. For example, as a student if you hand in work not for publication, you are unlikely to face legal trouble for plagiarism. Nevertheless, it may lead to severe consequences for your education, such as a failing grade, academic probation or even expulsion. On the other hand, if you intend to publish your work, plagiarism can destroy your reputation and have legal ramifications, because stealing copyright and intellectual property is against the law.

9.2.2 Academic Plagiarism: Types and Avoidance

Plagiarism means using others' work without giving them due credit. In academic writing, plagiarizing includes using words, ideas, or information from a source without correct citations, such as directly copying words or images, rephrasing sentences or passages, or co-opting someone else's ideas without citing the original work.

The following are common types of plagiarism in academic writing:

- Global plagiarism refers to plagiarizing a full text, including buying an essay or handing in an assignment done by someone else.
- Patchwork or mosaic plagiarism refers to copying phrases, passages, and ideas from various sources and compiling them into a new text.
- Incremental plagiarism refers to inserting a small amount of plagiarized content into a mostly original text.
- Self-plagiarism refers to recycling your prior work which has been submitted or published.

Besides text, you have to avoid plagiarizing things such as images, data, music, and art. Remember you must give credit to the source, whenever using something made by someone else.

Plagiarism often happens accidentally; therefore, it's easier to encounter plagiarism in academic writing. The following are certain common examples:

- Forgetting to use quotation marks for a quote;
- Paraphrasing too closely to the original text (e.g., only using several synonyms);
- Mentioning an idea that you read somewhere without citing it;
- Including the incorrect information in a citation;
- Including an incomplete reference list at the end of your paper. Even though done accidentally, it's still deemed plagiarism, and may cause severe consequences.

1. Self-plagiarism: Text Recycling

Self-plagiarism, or text recycling, refers to reusing textual material (prose, visuals, or equations) in a new document where (a) the material in the new document is the same as that of the source (or closely similar in both form and content), (b) the material is not presented in the new document as a citation (via quotation marks or block indentation), and (c) at least an author of the new document is also an author of the previous one.

Depending on contexts, text recycling can be either ethical, professionally accepted, legal, and even desirable for the communication of ideas, or unethical, professionally unaccepted, infringing copyright or violating a publishing contract and inhibiting communication. Hence, authors cannot be systematically prohibited or discouraged from recycling material from their previous work. Publishers, educational institutions and other organizations should make explicit and applicable guidelines for text recycling which can propel effective, ethical, and legal academic communication. Then authors can follow these rules for text recycling and carefully determine if the use of recycled material is legal and proper in its particular situation. Nevertheless, it is by no means easy to formulate such guidelines because of ethical and legal nuance and the contextual nature of text recycling.

2. How to Detect Plagiarism

Most academic institutions use a plagiarism checker tool to ensure the originality of submitted content. If the content is too similar to the content found by the checker, the author might be suspected of plagiarism. If you worry about unintentional plagiarism, you can run your content through a plagiarism checker on your own before submission. You can upload your document and the checker scans it, checking for any similarities to websites, journals, or other published sources within their database. The identified similarities will be shown in the form of a percentage when the scan is complete. Then you may scroll through, inserting citations if required. The accuracy of the results may vary due to the size of the database and the technological capabilities. Plagiarism checkers also vary in regard to privacy and confidentiality. In other words, some checkers, with a detailed privacy policy, commit to never sharing your data; whereas, others upload your data to an internal content database or share it with third parties.

3. How to Avoid Plagiarism

The safest way to prevent plagiarism is to cite all sources. However, you should also appropriately integrate them into your text by either quoting or rephrasing. Paraphrasing requires your complete understanding of the material, a full explanation of the author's main point in your own words and the citation of the source, instead of simply switching several words or using a few synonyms. When directly copying a phrase, sentence or passage from a source, use a quotation; in other words, quotation marks must be placed around the exact text you include from the source. Remember to integrate every quote in your own words, instead of using quotations as full sentences. As for common knowledge, you do not need to cite it, because it is commonly known and easily verified which you do not need to get from a specific source. For instance, no citation is required for the statement that Beijing is the capital city of the People's Republic of China, or the Nile is the world's longest river. Whereas, if you're uncertain if something is common knowledge, you may as well cite the source.

9.2.3 Errors in Published Scientific Writing

1. Error and Erratum

An error, being almost everywhere in the human world, occurs in academic publishing for various reasons, ranging from typographic errors to intentional misrepresentation of findings or results. Deliberate fraud is the most serious form of error in research, with data altered or even fabricated. These errors are handled differently, based on their severity, magnitude or willfulness.

An erratum is a correction of errors introduced to the article by the publisher. Publication of erratum notices is taken seriously, and verification will be sought by the publisher of the journal. Verification ranges from an author confirming that a mistake was made in the paper to a full investigation carried out by the author's institution or employer to ensure the study is fraudulent.

These errata usually arise as the result of a request from the author or an observation from a reviewer, editorial board member, another journal, a publisher, an employer, funder of research, a reader or "whistleblower," or a comparison of content using plagiarism software.

2. Types of Errors

For peer-reviewed content, errors can be classified into the following types.

1) Typographical: an error where a change of a word or a character would render the portion of the paper correct. If the context provides enough redundant information, the error can be easily corrected by the reader. It is important to fix these errors by errata lists and other means.

2) Slip: an error in a proof that might be fixed, although not conspicuously so. The claimed key theorem, in a slip, is either true or can be corrected with little cost.

3) Miscalculation: usually a sign or quantity error. In some circumstances the results are minor, and lead to better or worse results depending on the calculation.

4) Oversight or omission: stating a fact as true without enough folklore to support it. In some circumstances, the author believes the reader can provide such backup, so he/she omits it. More severely, the omission happens because the author believed the fact was true with an easy proof, when it may or may not be a fact and the author had a faulty argument causing him/her to reckon it true.

5) Major blunder: claiming a result that is true, and turns out not to be true in a socially accepted proof system.

3. Error Correction

Before turning in your work to the editor of an academic journal or press, you must proofread, edit and polish your scholarly writing. Remember the excellence of your text is vital to communicating explicitly and exactly with your audience and successfully getting publication. Be prepared that proofreading and editing processes tend to be far more complicated and time-consuming than your anticipation.

Minor typographical errors, such as spelling and grammar mistakes, can be corrected in the digital version of an article, often requiring no correction notice. Whereas, more significant errors, such as altering the order of authorship, adding information to the author note, replacing an entry in the reference list, and changing data or results, need the publisher not to merely fix the article but to make a correction notice: a formal, public announcement of the correction which informs readers of the changes to the published work. The notice can correct the knowledge base for present and future users of the information in the published article.

Inform the editor and publisher of the error, if you find any in your published article, with an online first article included. The editor and publisher will decide whether to issue a correction notice. If a notice is required, you are the one to write it, which outlines what the error was, what the correct information is, and if some or all versions of the original work have been fixed.

Once approved, the correction notice will appear in the journal's official template with the information given by the author. Usually, the notice is published with a DOI both in print and online and also attached to the article's record in research databases. In this way, readers will get it when they access the article or the database record for the article. In most cases, a corrected version of the article is also posted online and marked as being corrected on the first page.

The following are four common kinds of error correction:

- Erratum. If a substantive error is made by the journal which can influence the work or the reputation of authors, the notice issued is called erratum.
- Corrigendum. If a major error is made by the author(s), all the authors must approve and sign the corrigenda (corrections document) or the journal must be informed of their dissenting opinions.
- Retraction. If the results are found invalid, all coauthor(s) must sign a retraction that explicates the error and how it influenced the conclusions. This will be submitted for publication and is the most consequential error type.
- Addendum. If any additional information about a paper is published, it can include an Editorial Expression of Concern. It is appended to those papers that the editor thinks require additional explanation to be understood.

Review Questions

1. What are research ethics?
2. What are the principles of research ethics?
3. What are scientific misconducts?
4. What is plagiarism?
5. What is text recycling?
6. What are the common types of errors in scientific writing?

Bibliography

A Research Guide. 2022. What is a research paper outline and outline format. *A Research Guide for Students*. Retrieved April 21, 2022, from A Research Guide for Students website.

Academic Conferences International (ACI). 2021. Abstract guidelines for papers. *Academic Conferences International*. Retrieved September 26, 2021, from Academic Conferences International website.

Academic English UK. 2021. Academic English: A definition. *Academic English UK*. Retrieved January 23, 2021, from Academic Conferences International website.

Academic Journals. 2022. Accelerating discovery. *Academic Journals*. Retrieved May 26, 2022, from Academic Journals website.

Academic Journals. 2022. Journals by title. *Academic Journals*. Retrieved May 26, 2022, from Academic Journals website.

Adams, J. 2021. How to choose a paper topic. *wikiHow*. Retrieved April 23, 2021, from wikiHow website.

Adams, K. 2005. The sources of innovation and creativity. *Future Problem Solving Program International*. Retrieved May 26, 2022, from FPSPI website.

AIJR Publisher. 2021. Conference proceedings. *AIJR Publisher*. Retrieved April 22, 2021, from AIJR Publisher website.

AIMS. 2016. Why it's important for scientists to publish their work, and tips for submitting to F1000 Research. *Food and Agriculture Organization of he United Nations*. Retrieved April 22, 2022, from Food and Agriculture Organization of he United Nations website.

Aitchison, C. & Lee, A. 2006. Research writing: Problems and pedagogies. *Teaching in Higher Education*, *11*(3): 265–278.

Allan, B. 2010. *Study Skills Handbook*. *VDOCUMENT*. Retrieved April 20, 2021, from VDOCUMENT website.

Alston, J. M. 2019. What's the difference between a conference, a seminar, a workshop and a symposium? *Conference Monkey*. Retrieved April 25, 2021, from Conference Monkey website.

American Meteorological Society. 2022. References. *American Meteorological Society*. Retrieved May 21, 2022, from AMS website.

American Psychological Association. 2022. APA style: Correction notices. *American Psychological Association*. Retrieved May 31, 2022, from American Psychological Association website.

Andrade, C. 2011. How to write a good abstract for a scientific paper or conference presentation. *Indian Journal of Psychiatry, 53*(2): 172–175.

Andueza, A. 2019. Assessing academic writing: The construction and validation of an integrated task-based instrument to evaluate specific writing skills. *Relieve*, *25*(2): 1–20.

Anglia Ruskin University Library. 2022. ARU Harvard. *Anglia Ruskin University Library*. Retrieved May 21, 2022, from ARU University Library website.

Anstey, A. 2014. Writing style: What's in a title? *British Journal of Dermatology*, (170): 1003–1004.

Antoniou, M. & Moriarty, J. 2008. What can academic writers learn from creative writers? Developing Guidance and Support for Lecturers in Higher Education. *Teaching in Higher Education*, *13*(2): 157–167.

ASOC AIDU. 2021. What topics have you chosen for your research and why? *ASOC AIDU*. Retrieved April 23, 2021, from ASOC AIDU website.

Austin, K. 2019. The guide to technical report writing: How to do it properly based on 3 examples. *DoMyPapers*. Retrieved April 24, 2021, from DoMyPapers website.

Bachelor Print. 2022. Harvard referencing—Pros and cons & examples. *Bachelor Print*. Retrieved May 21, 2022, from Bachelor Print website.

Badley, G. 2009. Academic writing as shaping and re-shaping. *Teaching in Higher Education*, *14*(2): 209–219.

Bair, M. A. & Mader, C. E. 2013. Academic writing at the graduate level: Improving the curriculum through faculty collaboration. *Journal of University Teaching & Learning Practice*, *10*(1): 118–121.

Baker, C. 2017. How to write a conference abstract: A five-part plan for pitching your research at almost anything. *BAKERCATHERINE*. Retrieved April 23, 2021, from BAKERCATHERINE website.

Baumeister, R. F. & Leary, M. R. 1997. Writing narrative literature reviews. *Review of General Psychology*, (1): 311–320.

Berger, A. A. 2016. The academic writer's toolkit: A user's manual. *Taylor & Francis Group*. Retrieved April 23, 2021, from Taylor & Francis Group website.

Biggs, J., & Tang, C. 2011. *Teaching for Quality Learning at University*. Maidenhead: Open University Press.

BioScience Writers. 2019. Effective use of verb tense in scientific writing. *BioScience Writers*. Retrieved April 24, 2021, from BioScience Writers website.

Bit Academy. 2022. Technical report: What is it & how to write it? *BIT.AI Blog*. Retrieved April 15, 2022, from BIT.AI Blog website.

Boote, D. N. & Beile, P. 2005. Scholars before researchers: On the centrality of the dissertation literature review in research preparation. *Educational Researcher, 34*(6): 3–15.

Borja, A. 2021. 11 steps to structuring a science paper editors will take seriously. *Elsevier Connect*. Retrieved April 15, 2022, from Elsevier website.

Bright Hub Education. 2021. Proofreading & publishing: The final stage in the writing process for students with special needs. *Bright Hub Education*. Retrieved April 24, 2021, from Bright Hub Education website.

Burkill, S. & Burley, J. 1996. Getting started on a geography dissertation. *Journal of Geography in Higher Education*, (20): 431–437.

Calderon, J. 2021. Searching the scientific literature. *Humboldt State University*. Retrieved April 20, 2021, from Humboldt State University website.

Cambridge Dictionary. 2021. Literature. *Cambridge Dictionary*. Retrieved April 20, 2021, from Cambridge Dictionary website.

Caulfield, J. 2020. Writing a research paper introduction. *Scribbr.* Retrieved April 24, 2021, from Scribbr website.

Caulfield, J. 2022. Writing a research paper conclusion. *Scribbr.* Retrieved December 7, 2022, from Scribbr website.

Charles, J. 2021. Quick ways to choose a best topic for your thesis. *Best Essay Writing Service.* Retrieved April 23, 2021, from Best Essay Writing Service website.

Chiavolini, D. & Feinberg, J. S. 2018. Teaching research writing in academia. *American Medical Writers Association Journal (AMWA Journal), 33*(4): 180–183.

Cho, K., Cho, M. H. & Hacker, D. 2010. Self-monitoring support for learning to write. *Interactive Learning Environments, 18*(2): 101–113.

Cite This for Me. 2021. What are in-text citations? *Cite This for Me.* Retrieved April 24, 2021, from Cite This for Me website.

Clouser, C. 2021. Scientific literature and research at IUP. *Indiana University of Pennsylvania.* Retrieved April 20, 2021, from Indiana University of Pennsylvania website.

CQUniversity Library. 2021. Database searching. *CQUniversity Australia.* Retrieved April 24, 2021, from CQUniversity Australia website.

Creately. 2020. The ultimate 5-step writing process for all writers. *Creately.* Retrieved April 23, 2021, from Creately website.

Crossley, J. 2021. How to write the methodology chapter. *Grad Coach.* Retrieved April 24, 2021, from Grad Coach website.

Daly, P. 2016. What authors need to know about errata, expressions of concern, and retractions. *Editage Insights.* Retrieved May 31, 2022, from Editage Insights website.

Damme, H. V. 2016. Word usage in scientific writing. *Acta Chirurgica Belgica, 110*(2): 137.

Denicolo, P. & Becker, L. 2012. What is a research proposal? *Sage Publishing.* Retrieved April 23, 2021, from Sage Publishing website.

Denney, A. S. & Tewksbury, R. A. 2013. How to write a literature review. *Journal of Criminal Justice Education*, (24): 218–234.

Devitt, A. J. 2014. Genre pedagogies. In G. Tate, A. R. Taggart, K. Schick & H. B. Hessler (Eds.), *A Guide to Composition Pedagogies* (2nd ed.). New York: Oxford University Press, 146–162.

DifferenceBetween. 2022. Difference between symposium and conference. *DifferenceBetween*. Retrieved May 23, 2022, from DifferenceBetween website.

DOAJ. 2022. About DOAJ. *DOAJ Open Global Trusted*. Retrieved May 20, 2022, from DOAJ Open Global Trusted website.

Drubin, D. G. & Kellogg, D. R. 2012. English as universal language of science: Opportunities and challenges. *Molecular Biology of the Cell, 23*(8): 1399.

Ebeling, M. & Gibbs, J. 2007. Searching and reviewing the literature. *SAGE Publishing*. Retrieved May 20, 2022, from SAGE Publishing website.

EBSCO. 2018. What is the difference between academic journals and scholarly (peer-reviewed) journals? *EBSCO Connect*. Retrieved April 25, 2021, from EBSCO website.

EBSCO. 2022. About EBSCO. *EBSCO*. Retrieved May 20, 2022, from EBSCO website.

Elsevier Author Services. 2021. Why English is the language of science. *Elsevier*. Retrieved January 22, 2021, from Elsevier website.

Elsevier. 2022a. What is peer review? *Elsevier*. Retrieved May 26, 2022, from Elsevier website.

Elsevier. 2022b. Policy and best practice: Errata & corrigenda. *Elsevier*. Retrieved May 31, 2022, from Elsevier website.

Elton, L. 2010. Academic writing and tacit knowledge. *Teaching in Higher Education, 15*(2): 151–160.

Enago Academy. 2019. Thesis vs. dissertation—Know the difference and similarities! *Enago Academy*. Retrieved April 24, 2021, from Enago Academy website.

Enago Academy. 2021. 10 types of scientific misconduct. *Enago Academy*. Retrieved May 31, 2022, from Enago Academy website.

Enago Academy. 2022a. 8 most common types of plagiarism to stay away from! *Enago Academy*. Retrieved May 31, 2022, from Enago Academy website.

Enago Academy. 2022b. Fixing errors in a published paper: Tips for authors. *Enago Academy*. Retrieved May 31, 2022, from Enago Academy website.

Engber, D. 2013. How did English get to be the international language of science? *Popular Science, 283*(5): 72.

English for University. 2021. What is academic English? *English for University*. Retrieved January 23, 2021, from English for University website.

English Language Center. 2022. Harvard referencing guide. *The Hong Kong Polytechnic University*. Retrieved May 21, 2022, from the Hong Kong Polytechnic University website.

EssayTreasures. 2020. Types of literature review. *EssayTreasures*. Retrieved April 21, 2021, from EssayTreasures website.

eVenues. 2022. What is a seminar? *eVenues*. Retrieved May 23, 2022, from eVenues website.

Expert Journals. 2017. Tips for writing a great literature review format for academic articles. *Expert Journals*. Retrieved March 30, 2022, from Expert Journals website.

Fergie, G., Beeke, S., McKenna, C. & Creme, P. 2011. "It's a lonely walk": Supporting postgraduate researchers through writing. *International Journal of Teaching & Learning in Higher Education, 23*(2): 236–245.

FIS. The writing process—Publishing. *FIS.* Retrieved April 24, 2021, from FIS website.

Formplus. 2022. Peer review: Examples, journals & writing guide. *Formplus.* Retrieved May 26, 2022, from Formplus website.

FOURWAVES. 2022. The difference between a symposium and a conference. *FOURWAVES.* Retrieved May 23, 2022, from FOURWAVES website.

Foyewa, R. A. 2015. English: The international language of science and technology. *International Journal of English Language and Linguistics Research, 3*(5): 34–41.

French, A. 2018. "Fail better": Reconsidering the role of struggle and failure in academic writing development in higher education. *Innovations in Education and Teaching International, 55*(4): 408–416.

Gall, M. D., Borg, W. R. & Gall, J. P. 1996. *Education Research: An Introduction (6th ed.).* White Plains: Longman.

Georgia State University Library. 2021. Literature reviews: Types of literature. *Georgia State University.* Retrieved April 20, 2021, from Georgia State University website.

Godin, K., Stapleton, J., Kirkpatrick, S. I., Hanning, R. M. & Leatherdale, S. T. 2015. Applying systematic review search methods to the grey literature: A case study examining guidelines for school-based breakfast programs in Canada. *Systematic Review, 4*(1): 162–165.

Gopee, N. & Deane, M. 2013. Strategies for successful academic writing—institutional and non-institutional support for students. *Nurse Education Today, 33*(12): 1624–1631.

Green, B. N., Johnson, C. D. & Adams, A. 2006. Writing narrative literature reviews for peer-reviewed journals: Secrets of the trade. *Journal of Chiropractic Medicine, 5*(3): 101–117.

Gross, C. 2016. Scientific misconduct. *Annual Review Psychology,* (67): 693–711.

Hall, S. 2017. Definition of a research article. *Pen & the Pad.* Retrieved April 22, 2021, from Pen & the Pad website.

Hanna, M. 2019. Ethics of scientific writing. *Springer.* Retrieved May 31, 2022, from SpringerLink website.

Harris, S. 2022. What is the unity of a paragraph? *AuthorCast.* Retrieved October 23, 2022, from AuthorCast website.

Hart, C. 2002. *Doing a Literature Review: Releasing the Social Science Research Imagination.* London: Sage.

Harvard College Writing Center. 2022. Ending the essay: Conclusions. *Harvard University.* Retrieved April 24, 2022, from Harvard University website.

Hay, I. 2009. *Communication in Geography and the Environmental Sciences (3rd ed.).* Melbourne: Oxford University Press.

Hayward, A. 2017. Infographic: The secret to using tenses in scientific writing. *Editage Insights.* Retrieved April 24, 2021, from Editage Insights website.

Herrity, J. 2020. How to write a conclusion. *Indeed*. Retrieved April 24, 2021, from Indeed website.

Hertzberg, K. 2019. How to write an introduction. *Grammarly*. Retrieved April 24, 2021, from Grammarly website.

Hoffmann, R. 2015. Publishing scientific papers. *Cornell University*. Retrieved May 26, 2022, from Cornell University website.

Hundarenko, O. 2020. Students' perspectives on academic writing in European higher education (Based on 2019 Erasmus teaching experience in Slovak and Hungarian University). *Revista Romaneasca Pentru Educatie Multidimensionala, 12*(4): 87–102.

IEEE Xplore Digital Library. 2022. About IEEE Xplore. *IEEE Xplore*. Retrieved May 20, 2022, from IEEE Xplore website.

Illinois Library. 2022. Writing a research proposal. *Illinois University*. Retrieved April 3, 2022, from Illinois University website.

Imperial College London. 2022. Library services: Reference management. *Imperial College London.*Retrieved May 22, 2022, from Imperial College London website.

Indowhiz. 2019. Guideline for writing methodology in scientific papers. *Indowhiz*. Retrieved May 19, 2022, from Indowhiz website.

Iskander, J. K., Wolicki, S. B., Leeb, R. T. & Siegel, P. Z. 2018. Successful scientific writing and publishing: A step-by-step approach. *Tools and Techniques*, (15): 128–133.

Jaidka, K., Khoo, C. S. G. & Na, J. C. 2019. Characterizing human summarization strategies for text reuse and transformation in literature review writing. *Scientometrics*, (121): 1563–1582.

James, H. 2005. To attract or to inform: What are titles for? *Journal of Technical Writing and Communication*, (35): 203–213.

Jansen, D. 2020a. What (exactly) is a research proposal? *Grad Coach*. Retrieved April 3, 2022, from Grad Coach website.

Jansen, D. 2020b. What (exactly) is research methodology? *Grad Coach*. Retrieved April 24, 2021, from Grad Coach website.

Johnston, B. 2007. Methodological review: Mapping the literature in relation to the challenges for the non-participation project. *University of Southampton*. Retrieved April 24, 2021, from University of Southampton website.

Joseph, S. Stauffer Library. 2021. Types and conventions of science writing. *Queen's University*. Retrieved April 22, 2021, from Queen's University website.

JSTOR. 2022. About JSTOR. *JSTOR*. Retrieved May 20, 2022, from JSTOR website.

Juniper Publishers. 2021. Review article. *Juniper Publishers*. Retrieved April 24, 2021, from Juniper Publishers website.

Kim, Y. S. 2018. The importance of literature review in research writing. *Owlcation*. Retrieved April 20, 2021, from Owlcation website.

Kimmerly-Smith, J. 2021. How to format a scientific paper. *Scribendi*. Retrieved April 22, 2021, from Scribendi website.

Kirkwood Libraries. 2022. What are scholarly journal articles? *Kirkwood Community College*. Retrieved May 26, 2022, from Kirkwood Community College website.

Klassen, C. 2018. 5 steps of outlining an essay. *The University of British Columbia*. Retrieved April 21, 2022, from the University of British Columbia website.

Kluwer, W. 2016. Guidelines for young researchers on tackling common problems in scientific publishing. *Editage Insights*. Retrieved April 24, 2021, from Editage Insights website.

Kneale, P. 2012. *Study Skills for Geography, Earth & Environmental Students (3rd ed.)*. London: Hodder Education.

Kretser, A., Murphy, D., Bertuzzi, S., Abraham, T., Allison, D. B., Boor, K. J., Dwyer, J., Grantham, A., Harris, L. J., Hollander, R., Jacobs-Young, C., Rovito, S., Vafiadis, D., Woteki, C., Wyndham, J. & Yada, R. 2019. Scientific integrity principles and best practices: Recommendations from a scientific integrity consortium. *Science and Engineering Ethics*, (25): 327–355.

KU Writing Center. 2021. Original research. *The University of Kansas*. Retrieved April 22, 2021, from the University of Kansas website.

Kueffer, C. & Larson, B. M. H. 2014. Responsible use of language in scientific writing and science communication. *BioScience, 64*(8): 719–724.

Kumar, K. 2022. Scientific paper writing: Have you selected the right research question? *Cognibrain*. Retrieved May 31, 2022, from Cognibrain website.

Lamar Soutter Library. Scientific and scholarly writing. *UMass Medical School*. Retrieved April 24, 2021, from UMass Medical School website.

Lampi, J. P. & Reynolds, T. 2018. Connecting practice & research: From tacit to explicit disciplinary writing instruction. *Journal of Developmental Education, 41*(2): 26–28.

Last, S. 2021. *Technical Writing Essentials*. PRESSBOOKS. Retrieved April 24, 2021, from BCcampus website.

Lea, M. R. & Stierer, B. 2000. *Student Writing in Higher Education: New Contexts*. Buckingham: Open University Press.

LeCompte, M. D., Klinger, J. K., Campbell, S. A. & Menke, D. W. 2003. Editor's introduction. *Review of Educational Research, 73*(2), 123–124.

Life Persona. 2021. Scientific language: Characteristics, functions, types and examples. *Life Persona*. Retrieved April 24, 2021, from Life Persona website.

Light, R. J. & Pillemer, D. B. 1984. *Summing Up: The Science of Reviewing Research*. Cambridge: Harvard University Press.

Lindsay, S. 2015. What works for doctoral students in completing their thesis? *Teaching in Higher Education, 20*(2): 183–196.

Liu, X. 2017. Definition of research topic. *Sage Knowledge*. Retrieved April 23, 2021, from Sage

Knowledge website.

Mahood, Q., Van Eerd, D. & Irvin, E. 2014. Searching for grey literature for systematic reviews: Challenges and benefits. *Research Synthesis Methods, 5*(3): 221–234.

Majumder, K. 2019. 6 types of word choice errors in scientific writing. *Editage Insights*. Retrieved April 24, 2021, from Editage Insights website.

Martin, P. A. 1997. Writing a useful literature review for a quantitative research project. *Applied Nursing Research, 10*(3): 159–162.

Mayyasah, Q. 2020. What is scientific misconduct? *DISCOVERPHDS*. Retrieved May 31, 2022, from DISCOVERPHDS website.

McCombes, S. & George, T. 2022. How to write a research proposal. *Scribbr*. Retrieved December 7, 2022, from Scribbr website.

McCombes, S. 2019a. How to write a methodology. *Scribbr*. Retrieved April 24, 2021, from Scribbr website.

McCombes, S. 2019b. Quick guide to proofreading. *Scribbr*. Revised on March 28, 2022. Retrieved April 24, 2021, from Scribbr website.

McCombes, S. 2022. How to write a discussion section. *Scribbr*. Retrieved December 7, 2022, from Scribbr website.

McCurry, D. 2018. How to write an abstract for a conference. *ExOrdo*. Retrieved September 26, 2021, from ExOrdo website.

McCurry, D. 2019. Your complete guide to academic conferences. *ExOrdo*. Retrieved April 25, 2021, from ExOrdo website.

McMahon, P. 2011. Chinese voices: Chinese learners and their experiences of living and studying in the United Kingdom. *Journal of Higher Education Policy and Management, 33*(4): 401–414.

McMonigle, P. 2021. Conference proceedings. *PennState University Libraries*. Retrieved April 22, 2021, from PennState University Libraries website.

Melbourne University Library. 2021. Presenting and publishing at conferences. *The University of Melbourne*. Retrieved April 25, 2021, from the University of Melbourne website.

MIT Writing and Communication Center. 2021. Resources for writers: The writing process. *Massachusetts Institute of Technology*. Retrieved April 24, 2021, from MIT website.

Monash University Library. 2022. Citing and referencing: In-text citations. *Monash University*. Retrieved May 21, 2022, from Monash University website.

Monash University. 2021. Write like a pro. *Monash University*. Retrieved April 24, 2021, from Monash University website.

Morley, J. 2016. The academic phrasebank. *The University of Manchester*. Retrieved January 18, 2016, from the University of Manchester website.

Mudrak, B. 2021. Maintaining formal tone in scientific writing. *American Journal Experts*. Retrieved April 24, 2021, from AJE website.

National Center for Biotechnology Information. 2022. PubMed overview. *National Library of Medicine*. Retrieved May 20, 2022, from National Library of Medicine website.

NDSU Libraries. Finding and identifying original research articles in the sciences. *North Dakota State University*. Retrieved April 22, 2021, from North Dakota State University website.

Negretti, R. 2012. Metacognition in student academic writing: A longitudinal study of metacognitive awareness and its relation to task perception, self-regulation, and evaluation of performance. *Written Communication, 29*(2):142–179.

Nilson, L. B. 2013. *Creating Self-Regulated Learners: Strategies to Strengthen Students' Self-Awareness and Learning Skills*. Sterling: Stylus Publishing.

Nordquist, R. 2019. The drafting stage of the writing process. *ThoughtCo*. Retrieved April 24, 2021, from ThoughtCo website.

Nova, A. 2017. Learn how to write a literature review in simple steps. *MyPerfectWords*. Retrieved March 31, 2022, from MyPerfectWords website.

NSU Library. 2020. Research tips: Search strategy. *Nova Southeastern University*. Retrieved April 24, 2021, from Nova Southeastern University website.

OpenLab. Brainstorming, outlining, and organizing your paper. *New York City College of Technology*. Retrieved April 24, 2021, from New York City College of Technology website.

Paez, A. 2017. Grey literature: An important resource in systematic reviews. *Journal of Evidence-Based Medicine, 10*(3): 233–240.

Paperpile. 2021. Research and writing guides: The top list of academic research databases. *Paperpile*. Retrieved April 24, 2021, from Paperpile website.

Patterson, E. A. 2021. Reasons for publishing scientific papers. *Realize Engineering*. Retrieved April 25, 2021, from Realize Engineering website.

Paul, J. & Criado, A. R. 2020. The art of writing literature review: What do we know and what do we need to know? *International Business Review, 29*(4): 189–192.

PEDIAA. 2016. Difference Between Seminar and Conference. *PEDIAA*. Retrieved April 25, 2021, from PEDIAA website.

Pekrun, R., Goetz, T., Titz, W. & Perry, R. P. 2002. Academic emotions in students' self-regulated learning and achievement: A program of qualitative and quantitative research. *Educational Psychologist, 37*(2): 91–105.

Perelman, L. C., Paradis, J. & Barrett, E. 1998. *The Mayfield Handbook of Technical & Scientific Writing*. New York: McGraw-Hill.

Plagiarism. 2017. What is plagiarism? *Plagiarism*. Retrieved May 31, 2022, from Plagiarism website.

Pn, D. 2022. How to write a literature review. *EssayPro*. Retrieved March 30, 2022, from EssayPro website.

Prayag, A. 2019. Overview and principles of scientific writing. *Indian Journal of Medical and*

Paediatric Oncology, 40(3): 420–423.

Princeton University. 2021. Writing the introduction. *Princeton University*. Retrieved April 24, 2021, from Princeton University website.

Pro-Academic-Writers. 2020. How to create a successful research methodology. *Pro-Academic-Writers*. Retrieved April 24, 2021, from Pro-Academic-Writers website.

Proofed. 2021. 5 reasons the literature review is crucial to your paper. *Proofed*. Retrieved April 20, 2021, from Proofed website.

Proresearchpapers. 2022. Academic research databases in 2022: Top list to start your research. *Proresearchpapers*. Retrieved April 24, 2021, from Proresearchpapers website.

Purdue Online Writing Lab. 2021. Research and citation. *Purdue University*. Retrieved April 21, 2021, from Purdue University website.

Purdue Online Writing Lab. 2021a. The writing process. *Purdue University*. Retrieved April 24, 2021, from Purdue University website.

Purdue Online Writing Lab. 2021b. Writing a research paper. *Purdue University*. Retrieved April 23, 2021, from Purdue University website.

Randolph, J. 2009. A guide to writing the dissertation literature review. *Practical Assessment, Research, and Evaluation, 14*(13): 67–69.

Randolph, J. J., Griffin, A. E., Zeiger, S. R., Falbe, K. N., Freeman, N. A., Taylor, B. E., Westbrook, A. F., Lico, C. C., Starling, C. N., Sprull, N. M., Holt, C., Smith, K. & McAnespie, H. 2013. A methodological review of the articles publishes in georgia educational researcher from 2003–2010. *Georgia Educational Researcher, 10*(1): 83–87.

Readingcraze. 2013. What are the qualities of a good research topic. *Readingcraze*. Retrieved April 15, 2022, from Readingcraze website.

Research Prospect. 2021. Research methodology. *Research Prospect*. Retrieved April 24, 2021, from Research Prospect website.

Resnik, D. B. 2020. What is ethics in research & why is it important? *National Institute of Environmental Health Sciences*. Retrieved May 31, 2022, from NIH website.

Rewhorn, S. 2018. Writing your successful literature review. *Journal of Geography in Higher Education, 42*(1): 143–147.

Ridley, D. 2012. *The Literature Review: A Step-by Step Guide for Students*. London: Sage.

Sacred Heart University Library. 2021. Organizing academic research papers: Choosing a title. *Sacred Heart University*. Retrieved April 23, 2021, from Sacred Heart University website.

SAGE Publishing. 2019. Conducting a literature review. *SAGE Publishing*. Retrieved April 20, 2021, from SAGE Publishing website.

Sallee, M., Hallett, R. & Tierney, W. 2011. Teaching writing in graduate school. *College Teaching, 59*(2): 66–72.

Sam, A. 2016. 10 functions of language in linguistics. *Notes Read*. Retrieved April 24, 2021, from Notes Read website.

Santelmann, L. M., Stevens, D. D. & Martin, S. B. 2018. Fostering master's students' metacognition and self-regulation practices for research writing. *College Teaching, 66*(3): 111–123.

Santiago Canyon College Library. Scholarly journals. *Santiago Canyon College*. Retrieved May 26, 2022, from Santiago Canyon College website.

Schumann, H., Berres, A., Stehr, T. & Engelhardt, D. 2020. Effective selection of quality literature during a systematic literature review. *Informing Science: The International Journal of an Emerging Transdiscipline, 23*: 77–87.

ScienceDirect. 2021. Peer review. *ScienceDirect*. Retrieved April 25, 2021, from ScienceDirect website.

ScienceDirect. 2022. Web of Science. *ScienceDirect*. Retrieved May 20, 2022, from ScienceDirect website.

Scribbr. 2022. Plagiarism. *Scribbr*. Retrieved May 31, 2022, from Scribbr website.

SFU Library. 2021. Grey literature: What it is & how to find it. *Simon Fraser University*. Retrieved April 24, 2021, from Simon Fraser University website.

SFU Library. 2021. What is a scholarly (or peer-reviewed) journal? *Simon Fraser University*. Retrieved April 25, 2021, from Simon Fraser University website.

Shaikh, A. A. 2016. 7 steps to publishing in a scientific journal. *Elsevier*. Retrieved April 25, 2021, from Elsevier website.

Sheffield, N. 2011. Passive voice in scientific writing. *Duke University Graduate School*. Retrieved April 24, 2021, from Duke University Graduate School website.

Singleton-Jackson, J. & Lumsden, D. B. 2009. Johnny still can't write, even if he goes to college: A study of writing proficiency in higher education graduate students. *Current Issues in Education, 121*(10): 1–39.

SkillsYouNeed. 2022. Ethical issues in research. *SkillsYouNeed*. Retrieved May 31, 2022, from SkillsYouNeed website.

Snyder, H. 2019. Literature review as a research methodology: An overview and guidelines. *Journal of Business Research, 104*: 333–339.

Sonntag, A. 2021. How to write a good abstract for a conference paper. *University Association for Contemporary European Studies*. Retrieved September 26, 2021, from University Association for Contemporary European Studies website.

Southwestern University. 2022. Benefits of peer review. *Southwestern University*. Retrieved May 26, 2022, from Southwestern University website.

Spacey, J. 2018. 7 examples of original research. *Simplicable*. Retrieved May 22, 2022, from Simplicable website.

Springer. 2022. About Springer. *Springer*. Retrieved May 20, 2022, from Springer website.

StackExchange. 2022a. How do I fix someone's published error? *StackExchange*. Retrieved May 31, 2022, from StackExchange website.

StackExchange. 2022b. What is done in a workshop? *StackExchange.* Retrieved May 23, 2022, from StackExchange website.

Sudheesh, K., Duggappa, D. R. & Nethra, S. S. 2016. How to write a research proposal? *Indian Journal of Anaesthesia, 60*(9): 631–634.

SUNY Geneseo's Writing Guide. Grammar and usage. *The State University of New York.* Retrieved April 24, 2021, from the State University of New York website.

Surbhi, S. 2019. Difference between reference and bibliography. *Key Differences.* Retrieved May 22, 2022, from Key Differences website.

Swoger, B. J. M. 2021. A very brief introduction to the scientific literature. *The Undergraduate Science Librarian.* Retrieved January 25, 2021, from the Undergraduate Science Librarian website.

Tardy, C. 2004. The role of English in scientific communication: Lingua fanca or Tyrannosaurus rex? *Journal of English for Academic Purposes, 3*: 247–269.

Taylor & Francis Author Services. 2021. What is a review article? *Taylor & Francis Author Services.* Retrieved September 21, 2021, from Taylor & Francis Author Services website.

Taylor, E. 2021. How to write the methodology for a dissertation. *Ivory Research.* Retrieved April 24, 2021, from Ivory Research website.

Tetzner, R. 2021a. How to write a journal article. *Journal-publishing.* Retrieved April 21, 2022, from Journal-publishing website.

Tetzner, R. 2021b. Revisons and errors in journal articles. *Journal-publishing.* Retrieved May 31, 2022, from Journal-publishing website.

Texas A&M University Libraries. 2021. What is a technical report? *Texas A&M University.* Retrieved April 22, 2021, from Texas A&M University website.

Text Recycling Research Project. What is text recycling? *Text Recycling Research Project.* Retrieved May 31, 2022, from the Text Recycling Research Project website.

The Best Master's Degrees. 2021. What is the difference between a thesis and a dissertation? *The Best Master's Degrees.* Retrieved April 22, 2021, from the Best Master's Degrees website.

The Glossary of Education Reform. 2021. Academic language. *The Glossary of Education Reform.* Retrieved January 23, 2021, from the Glossary of Education Reform website.

The Institution of Engineering and Technology. 2022. A guide to technical report writing. *The Institution of Engineering and Technology.* Retrieved April 15, 2022, from the Institution of Engineering and Technology website.

The New York Academy of Medicine. 2016. What is grey literature? *Grey Literature Report.* Retrieved April 24, 2021, from Grey Literature Report website.

The University of British Columbia. 2022a. STEM writing resources for learning (ScWRL). *The University of British Columbia.* Retrieved April 24, 2022, from the University of British Columbia website.

The University of British Columbia. 2022b. Structure of theses and dissertations. *The University of British Columbia*. Retrieved April 14, 2022, from the University of British Columbia website.

The University of Cambridge. 2021. Engineering library: Literature searching and reviewing. *The University of Cambridge*. Retrieved April 24, 2021, from the University of Cambridge website.

The University of Minnesota Libraries Publishing. 2021. Writing for success. *University of Minnesota*. Retrieved April 21, 2021, from University of Minnesota website.

The Writing Center. 2018. How to write a research question. *George Mason University*. Retrieved April 23, 2021, from George Mason University website.

The Writing Center. 2021. Writing an abstract for your research paper. *University of Wisconsin-Madison*. Retrieved April 24, 2021, from University of Wisconsin-Madison website.

The Writing Center. 2022. Introductions. *The University of North Carolina at Chaple Hill*. Retrieved April 22, 2022, from the University of North Carolina at Chaple Hill website.

Time4writing. How to write a good conclusion paragraph. *Time4writing*. Retrieved April 24, 2021, from Time4writing website.

Tranfield, D., Denyer, D. & Smart, P. 2003. Towards a methodology for developing evidence-informed management knowledge by means of systematic review. *British Journal of Management, 14*: 207–222.

UEFAP. 2021.What is EAP? *Using English for Academic Purposes (UEFAP)*. Retrieved January 25, 2021, from UEFAP website.

University Libraries. 2021. How to conduct a literature review: Types of literature reviews. *University of Alabama*. Retrieved April 21, 2021, from University of Alabama website.

University of Bristol. 2022. A guide to referencing academic work. *University of Bristol*. Retrieved May 21, 2022, from University of Bristol website.

University of Leeds. 2021. Literature searching explained. *University of Leeds*. Retrieved April 24, 2021, from University of Leeds website.

University of Nottingham. 2021. Why do we write? *University of Nottingham*. Retrieved January 23, 2021, from University of Nottingham website.

University of Reading. 2022a. APA referencing. *University of Reading*. Retrieved May 21, 2022, from University of Reading website.

University of Reading. 2022b. Citing references. *University of Reading*. Retrieved May 21, 2022, from University of Reading website.

University of Saint Mary. 2022. Tools for effective writing. *University of Saint Mary*. Retrieved May 22, 2022, from University of Saint Mary website.

University of the People. 2021. Dissertation vs thesis: The differences that matter. *University of the People*. Retrieved October 9, 2021, from University of the People website.

University of Toronto. 2022. Engineering graduate studies: Research methods. *University of Toronto*. Retrieved April 22, 2022, from University of Toronto website.

UNSW Sydney. 2022. The footnote/bibliography referencing system. *UNSW Sydney*. Retrieved May 22, 2022, from UNSW Sydney website.

Unwin, G., Tucker, D. H. & Unwin, P. S. 2020. History of publishing. *Encyclopedia Britannica*. Retrieved April 24, 2021, from Encyclopedia Britannica website.

USC Libraries. 2021a. Research guides. *University of Southern California*. Retrieved April 23, 2021, from University of Southern California website.

USC Libraries. 2021b. Research guides: Organizing your social sciences research paper. *University of Southern California*. Retrieved April 24, 2021, from University of Southern California website.

USDA. 2022. Scientific integrity and research misconduct. *U.S. Department of Agriculture (USDA)*. Retrieved May 31, 2022, from USDA website.

VeQuill. 2021. What are the different functions of language? *VeQuill*. Retrieved April 24, 2021, from VeQuill website.

Verhoef, M. J. 2004. Writing an effective research proposal. *University of Calgary*. Retrieved April 24, 2022, from University of Calgary website.

Villavicencio, F. T. & Bernardo, A. B. I. 2013. Positive academic emotions moderate the relationship between self-regulation and academic achievement. *British Journal of Educational Psychology, 83*(2): 329–340.

Walden University. 2022a. What is an in-text citation? *Walden University*. Retrieved May 21, 2022, from Walden University website.

Walden University. 2022b. Writing a paper. *Walden University*. Retrieved April 24, 2022, from Walden University website.

Wang, Y., Fang, Q. & Peng, W. 2018. China's recently launched English-language science and technology journals, 2012–2016. *Journal of Scholarly Publishing, 50*(1): 37–47.

Wellington, J. 2010. More than a matter of cognition: An exploration of affective writing problems of post-graduate students and their possible solutions. *Teaching in Higher Education, 15*(2): 135–150.

WikiHow. 2020. How to write research methodology. *WikiHow*. Retrieved April 24, 2021, from WikiHow website.

WikiHow. 2021. How to publish a book. *WikiHow*. Retrieved April 24, 2021, from WikiHow website.

WikiHow. 2022. How to prepare a workshop. *WikiHow*. Retrieved May 23, 2022, from WikiHow website.

Wiley. 2022. Wiley online library. *Wiley*. Retrieved May 20, 2022, from Wiley website.

Wolters, C. A. 2003. Understanding procrastination from a self-regulated learning perspective.

Journal of Educational Psychology, 95(1): 179–187.

Write like a Scientist. 2021. A guide to scientific communication: By genre. *Write like a Scientist.* Retrieved April 22, 2021, from Write like a Scientist website.